SQL Performance Explained

Markus Winand

Publisher:
Markus Winand

Maderspergerstasse 1-3/9/11
1160 Wien
AUSTRIA
<office@winand.at>

Copyright © 2012–2018 Markus Winand

All rights reserved. No part of this publication may be reproduced, stored, or transmitted in any form or by any means — electronic, mechanical, photocopying, recording, or otherwise — without the prior consent of the publisher.

Many of the names used by manufacturers and sellers to distinguish their products are trademarked. Wherever such designations appear in this book, and we were aware of a trademark claim, the names have been printed in all caps or initial caps.

While every precaution has been taken in the preparation of this book, the publisher and author assume no responsibility for errors and omissions, or for damages resulting from the use of the information contained herein.

The book solely reflects the author's views. The database vendors mentioned have neither supported the work financially nor verified the content.

Printed in Austria:
DGS - Druck- u. Graphikservice GmbH — Wien — Austria

Cover design:
tomasio.design — Mag. Thomas Weninger — Wien — Austria

Cover photo:
Brian Arnold — Turriff — UK

Copy editor:
Nathan Ingvalson — Graz — Austria

ISBN: 978-3-9503078-2-5
German edition: 978-3-9503078-1-8   Japanese edition: 978-3-9503078-4-9
French edition: 978-3-9503078-3-2   Spanish edition: 978-3-9503078-5-6

2018-05-01

SQL Performance Explained

*Everything developers need to
know about SQL performance*

Markus Winand
Vienna, Austria

CONTENTS

Preface vi

1. Anatomy of an Index 1
   The Index Leaf Nodes 2
   The Search Tree (B-Tree) 4
   Slow Indexes, Part I 6

2. The Where Clause 9
   The Equality Operator 9
      Primary Keys 10
      Concatenated Indexes 12
      Slow Indexes, Part II 18
   Functions 24
      Case-Insensitive Search Using UPPER or LOWER 24
      User-Defined Functions 29
      Over-Indexing 31
   Parameterized Queries 32
   Searching for Ranges 39
      Greater, Less and BETWEEN 39
      Indexing LIKE Filters 45
      Index Merge 49
   Partial Indexes 51
   NULL in the Oracle Database 53
      Indexing NULL 54
      NOT NULL Constraints 56
      Emulating Partial Indexes 60
   Obfuscated Conditions 62
      Date Types 62
      Numeric Strings 68
      Combining Columns 70
      Smart Logic 72
      Math 77

IV

SQL PERFORMANCE EXPLAINED

3. Performance and Scalability 79
    Performance Impacts of Data Volume 80
    Performance Impacts of System Load 85
    Response Time and Throughput 87

4. The Join Operation 91
    Nested Loops 92
    Hash Join 101
    Sort Merge 109

5. Clustering Data 111
    Index Filter Predicates Used Intentionally 112
    Index-Only Scan 116
    Index-Organized Tables 122

6. Sorting and Grouping 129
    Indexing Order By 130
    Indexing ASC, DESC and NULLS FIRST/LAST 134
    Indexing Group By 139

7. Partial Results 143
    Querying Top-N Rows 143
    Paging Through Results 147
    Using Window Functions for Pagination 156

8. Modifying Data 159
    Insert 159
    Delete 162
    Update 163

A. Execution Plans 165
    Oracle Database 166
    PostgreSQL 172
    SQL Server 180
    MySQL 188

Index 193

PREFACE

DEVELOPERS NEED TO INDEX

SQL performance problems are as old as SQL itself—some might even say that SQL is inherently slow. Although this might have been true in the early days of SQL, it is definitely not true anymore. Nevertheless SQL performance problems are still commonplace. How does this happen?

The SQL language is perhaps the most successful fourth-generation programming language (4GL). Its main benefit is the capability to separate *"what"* and *"how"*. An SQL statement is a straight description *what* is needed without instructions as to *how* to get it done. Consider the following example:

```
SELECT date_of_birth
  FROM employees
 WHERE last_name = 'WINAND'
```

The SQL query reads like an English sentence that explains the requested data. Writing SQL statements generally does not require any knowledge about inner workings of the database or the storage system (such as disks, files, etc.). There is no need to tell the database which files to open or how to find the requested rows. Many developers have years of SQL experience yet they know very little about the processing that happens in the database.

The separation of concerns—what is needed versus how to get it—works remarkably well in SQL, but it is still not perfect. The abstraction reaches its limits when it comes to performance: the author of an SQL statement by definition does not care *how* the database executes the statement. Consequently, the author is not responsible for slow execution. However, experience proves the opposite; i.e., the author must know a little bit about the database to prevent performance problems.

It turns out that the only thing *developers* need to learn is how to index. Database indexing is, in fact, a development task. That is because the most important information for proper indexing is not the storage system configuration or the hardware setup. The most important information for indexing is how the application queries the data. This knowledge—about

VI

the access path — is not very accessible to database administrators (DBAs) or external consultants. Quite some time is needed to gather this information through reverse engineering of the application: development, on the other hand, has that information anyway.

This book covers everything developers need to know about indexes — and nothing more. To be more precise, the book covers the most important index type only: the *B-tree index*.

The B-tree index works almost identically in many databases. The book only uses the terminology of the Oracle® database, but the principles apply to other databases as well. Side notes provide relevant information for MySQL, PostgreSQL and SQL Server®.

The structure of the book is tailor-made for developers; most chapters correspond to a particular part of an SQL statement.

CHAPTER 1 - ANATOMY OF AN INDEX
The first chapter is the only one that doesn't cover SQL specifically; it is about the fundamental structure of an index. An understanding of the index structure is essential to following the later chapters — don't skip this!

Although the chapter is rather short — only about eight pages — after working through the chapter you will already understand the phenomenon of slow indexes.

CHAPTER 2 - THE WHERE CLAUSE
This is where we pull out all the stops. This chapter explains all aspects of the where clause, from very simple single column lookups to complex clauses for ranges and special cases such as LIKE.

This chapter makes up the main body of the book. Once you learn to use these techniques, you will write much faster SQL.

CHAPTER 3 - PERFORMANCE AND SCALABILITY
This chapter is a little digression about performance measurements and database scalability. See why adding hardware is not the best solution to slow queries.

CHAPTER 4 - THE JOIN OPERATION
Back to SQL: here you will find an explanation of how to use indexes to perform a fast table join.

PREFACE: DEVELOPERS NEED TO INDEX

CHAPTER 5 - CLUSTERING DATA
> Have you ever wondered if there is any difference between selecting a single column or all columns? Here is the answer—along with a trick to get even better performance.

CHAPTER 6 - SORTING AND GROUPING
> Even **order by** and **group by** can use indexes.

CHAPTER 7 - PARTIAL RESULTS
> This chapter explains how to benefit from a "pipelined" execution if you don't need the full result set.

CHAPTER 8 - INSERT, DELETE AND UPDATE
> How do indexes affect write performance? Indexes don't come for free—use them wisely!

APPENDIX A - EXECUTION PLANS
> Asking the database how it executes a statement.

CHAPTER 1

ANATOMY OF AN INDEX

"An index makes the query fast" is the most basic explanation of an index I have ever seen. Although it describes the most important aspect of an index very well, it is—unfortunately—not sufficient for this book. This chapter describes the index structure in a less superficial way but doesn't dive too deeply into details. It provides just enough insight for one to understand the SQL performance aspects discussed throughout the book.

An index is a distinct structure in the database that is built using the `create index` statement. It requires its own disk space and holds a copy of the indexed table data. That means that an index is pure redundancy. Creating an index does not change the table data; it just creates a new data structure that refers to the table. A database index is, after all, very much like the index at the end of a book: it occupies its own space, it is highly redundant, and it refers to the actual information stored in a different place.

CLUSTERED INDEXES

SQL Server and MySQL (using InnoDB) take a broader view of what *"index"* means. They refer to tables that consist of the index structure only as *clustered indexes*. These tables are called Index-Organized Tables (IOT) in the Oracle database.

Chapter 5, *"Clustering Data"*, describes them in more detail and explains their advantages and disadvantages.

Searching in a database index is like searching in a printed telephone directory. The key concept is that all entries are arranged in a well-defined order. Finding data in an ordered data set is fast and easy because the sort order determines each entry's position.

1

CHAPTER 1: ANATOMY OF AN INDEX

A database index is, however, more complex than a printed directory because it undergoes constant change. Updating a printed directory for every change is impossible for the simple reason that there is no space between existing entries to add new ones. A printed directory bypasses this problem by only handling the accumulated updates with the next printing. An SQL database cannot wait that long. It must process **insert**, **delete** and **update** statements immediately, keeping the index order without moving large amounts of data.

The database combines two data structures to meet the challenge: a doubly linked list and a search tree. These two structures explain most of the database's performance characteristics.

THE INDEX LEAF NODES

The primary purpose of an index is to provide an ordered representation of the indexed data. It is, however, not possible to store the data sequentially because an **insert** statement would need to move the following entries to make room for the new one. Moving large amounts of data is very time-consuming so the **insert** statement would be very slow. The solution to the problem is to establish a logical order that is independent of physical order in memory.

The logical order is established via a doubly linked list. Every node has links to two neighboring entries, very much like a chain. New nodes are inserted between two existing nodes by updating their links to refer to the new node. The physical location of the new node doesn't matter because the doubly linked list maintains the logical order.

The data structure is called a *doubly linked list* because each node refers to the preceding and the following node. It enables the database to read the index forwards or backwards as needed. It is thus possible to insert new entries without moving large amounts of data—it just needs to change some pointers.

Doubly linked lists are also used for collections (containers) in many programming languages.

2

THE INDEX LEAF NODES

Programming Language	Name
Java	java.util.LinkedList
.NET Framework	System.Collections.Generic.LinkedList
C++	std::list

Databases use doubly linked lists to connect the so-called index *leaf nodes*. Each leaf node is stored in a *database block* or *page*; that is, the database's smallest storage unit. All index blocks are of the same size—typically a few kilobytes. The database uses the space in each block to the extent possible and stores as many index entries as possible in each block. That means that the index order is maintained on two different levels: the index entries within each leaf node, and the leaf nodes among each other using a doubly linked list.

Figure 1.1. Index Leaf Nodes and Corresponding Table Data

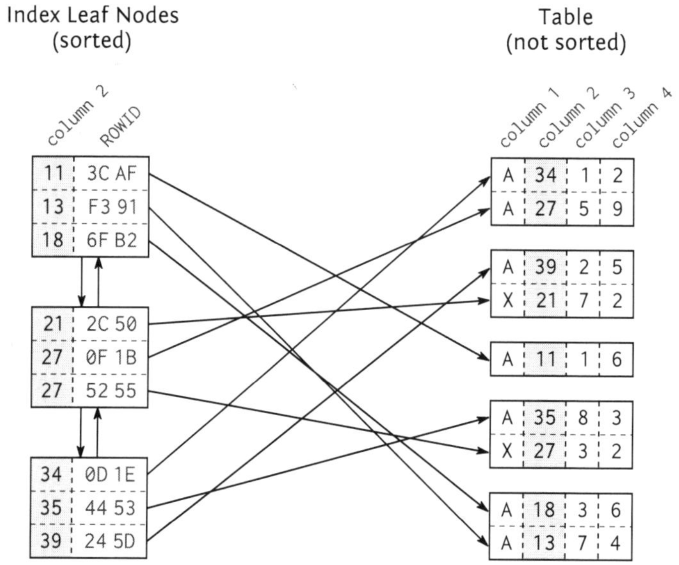

Figure 1.1 illustrates the index leaf nodes and their connection to the table data. Each index entry consists of the indexed columns (the key, column 2) and refers to the corresponding table row (via ROWID or RID). Unlike the index, the table data is stored in a heap structure and is not sorted at all. There is neither a relationship between the rows stored in the same table block nor is there any connection between the blocks.

3

CHAPTER 1: ANATOMY OF AN INDEX

THE SEARCH TREE (B-TREE)

The index leaf nodes are stored in an arbitrary order—the position on the disk does not correspond to the logical position according to the index order. It is like a telephone directory with shuffled pages. If you search for "Smith" but first open the directory at "Robinson", it is by no means granted that Smith follows Robinson. A database needs a second structure to find the entry among the shuffled pages quickly: a *balanced search tree*—in short: the B-tree.

Figure 1.2. B-tree Structure

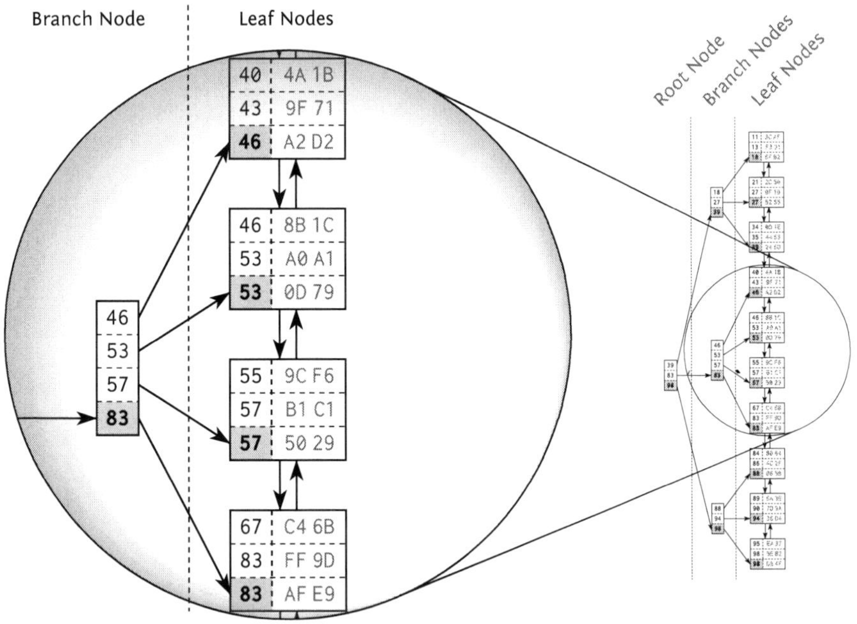

Figure 1.2 shows an example index with 30 entries. The doubly linked list establishes the logical order between the leaf nodes. The root and branch nodes support quick searching among the leaf nodes.

The figure highlights a branch node and the leaf nodes it refers to. Each branch node entry corresponds to the biggest value in the respective leaf node. Take the first leaf node as an example: the biggest value in this node is 46, which is thus stored in the corresponding branch node entry. The same is true for the other leaf nodes so that in the end the branch node

4

THE SEARCH TREE (B-TREE)

has the values 46, 53, 57 and 83. According to this scheme, a branch layer is built up until all the leaf nodes are covered by a branch node.

The next layer is built similarly, but on top of the first branch node level. The procedure repeats until all keys fit into a single node, the *root node*. The structure is a *balanced search tree* because the tree depth is equal at every position; the distance between root node and leaf nodes is the same everywhere.

> **NOTE**
>
> A B-tree is a balanced tree—not a binary tree.

Once created, the database maintains the index automatically. It applies every **insert**, **delete** and **update** to the index and keeps the tree in balance, thus causing maintenance overhead for write operations. Chapter 8, *"Modifying Data"*, explains this in more detail.

Figure 1.3. B-Tree Traversal

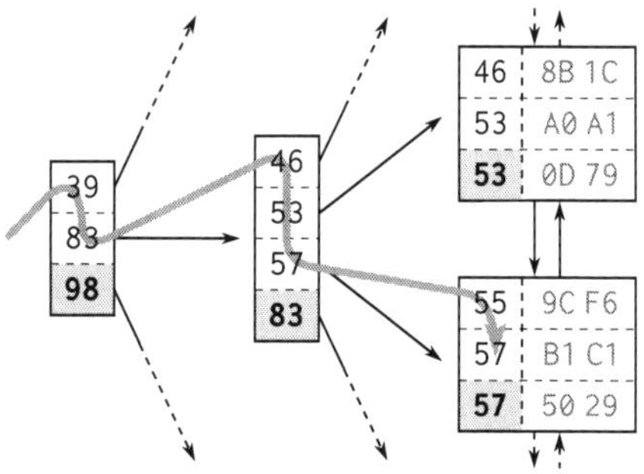

46	8B 1C
53	A0 A1
53	0D 79

55	9C F6
57	B1 C1
57	50 29

39
83
98

46
53
57
83

Figure 1.3 shows an index fragment to illustrate a search for the key "57". The tree traversal starts at the root node on the left-hand side. Each entry is processed in ascending order until a value is greater than or equal to (>=) the search term (57). In the figure it is the entry 83. The database follows the reference to the corresponding branch node and repeats the procedure until the tree traversal reaches a leaf node.

> **IMPORTANT**
>
> The B-tree enables the database to find a leaf node quickly.

The tree traversal is a very efficient operation—so efficient that I refer to it as the *first power of indexing*. It works almost instantly—even on a huge data set. That is primarily because of the tree balance, which allows accessing all elements with the same number of steps, and secondly because of the logarithmic growth of the tree depth. That means that the tree depth grows very slowly compared to the number of leaf nodes. Real world indexes with millions of records have a tree depth of four or five. A tree depth of six is hardly ever seen. The box "Logarithmic Scalability" describes this in more detail.

SLOW INDEXES, PART I

Despite the efficiency of the tree traversal, there are still cases where an index lookup doesn't work as fast as expected. This contradiction has fueled the myth of the *"degenerated index"* for a long time. The myth proclaims an index rebuild as the miracle solution. The real reason trivial statements can be slow—even when using an index—can be explained on the basis of the previous sections.

The first ingredient for a slow index lookup is the leaf node chain. Consider the search for "57" in Figure 1.3 again. There are obviously two matching entries in the index. At least two entries are the same, to be more precise: the next leaf node could have further entries for "57". The database *must* read the next leaf node to see if there are any more matching entries. That means that an index lookup not only needs to perform the tree traversal, it also needs to follow the leaf node chain.

The second ingredient for a slow index lookup is accessing the table. Even a single leaf node might contain many hits—often hundreds. The corresponding table data is usually scattered across many table blocks (see Figure 1.1, "Index Leaf Nodes and Corresponding Table Data"). That means that there is an additional table access for each hit.

An index lookup requires three steps: (1) the tree traversal; (2) following the leaf node chain; (3) fetching the table data. The tree traversal is the only step that has an upper bound for the number of accessed blocks—the index depth. The other two steps might need to access many blocks—they cause a slow index lookup.

6

LOGARITHMIC SCALABILITY

In mathematics, the logarithm of a number to a given base is the power or exponent to which the base must be raised in order to produce the number [Wikipedia[1]].

In a search tree the base corresponds to the number of entries per branch node and the exponent to the tree depth. The example index in Figure 1.2 holds up to four entries per node and has a tree depth of three. That means that the index can hold up to 64 (4^3) entries. If it grows by one level, it can already hold 256 entries (4^4). Each time a level is *added*, the maximum number of index entries *quadruples*. The logarithm reverses this function. The tree depth is therefore $\log_4$(number-of-index-entries).

The logarithmic growth enables the example index to search a million records with ten tree levels, but a real world index is even more efficient. The main factor that affects the tree depth, and therefore the lookup performance, is the number of entries in each tree node. This number corresponds to—mathematically speaking—the basis of the logarithm. The higher the basis, the shallower the tree, the faster the traversal.

Tree Depth	Index Entries
3	64
4	256
5	1,024
6	4,096
7	16,384
8	65,536
9	262,144
10	1,048,576

Databases exploit this concept to a maximum extent and put as many entries as possible into each node—often hundreds. That means that every new index level supports a hundred times more entries.

---

[1] http://en.wikipedia.org/wiki/Logarithm

The origin of the "slow indexes" myth is the misbelief that an index lookup just traverses the tree, hence the idea that a slow index must be caused by a "broken" or "unbalanced" tree. The truth is that you can actually ask most databases how they use an index. The Oracle database is rather verbose in this respect and has three distinct operations that describe a basic index lookup:

INDEX UNIQUE SCAN

> The INDEX UNIQUE SCAN performs the tree traversal only. The Oracle database uses this operation if a unique constraint ensures that the search criteria will match no more than one entry.

INDEX RANGE SCAN

> The INDEX RANGE SCAN performs the tree traversal *and* follows the leaf node chain to find all matching entries. This is the fallback operation if multiple entries could possibly match the search criteria.

TABLE ACCESS BY INDEX ROWID

> The TABLE ACCESS BY INDEX ROWID operation retrieves the row from the table. This operation is (often) performed for every matched record from a preceding index scan operation.

The important point is that an INDEX RANGE SCAN can potentially read a large part of an index. If there is one more table access for each row, the query can become slow even when using an index.

CHAPTER 2

THE WHERE CLAUSE

The previous chapter described the structure of indexes and explained the cause of poor index performance. In the next step we learn how to spot and avoid these problems in SQL statements. We start by looking at the **where** clause.

The **where** clause defines the search condition of an SQL statement, and it thus falls into the core functional domain of an index: finding data quickly. Although the **where** clause has a huge impact on performance, it is often phrased carelessly so that the database has to scan a large part of the index. The result: a poorly written **where** clause is the first ingredient of a slow query.

This chapter explains how different operators affect index usage and how to make sure that an index is usable for as many queries as possible. The last section shows common anti-patterns and presents alternatives that deliver better performance.

THE EQUALITY OPERATOR

The equality operator is both the most trivial and the most frequently used SQL operator. Indexing mistakes that affect performance are still very common and **where** clauses that combine multiple conditions are particularly vulnerable.

This section shows how to verify index usage and explains how concatenated indexes can optimize combined conditions. To aid understanding, we will analyze a slow query to see the real world impact of the causes explained in Chapter 1.

9

Primary Keys

We start with the simplest yet most common **where** clause: the primary key lookup. For the examples throughout this chapter we use the EMPLOYEES table defined as follows:

```
CREATE TABLE employees (
    employee_id    NUMBER          NOT NULL,
    first_name     VARCHAR2(1000) NOT NULL,
    last_name      VARCHAR2(1000) NOT NULL,
    date_of_birth DATE            NOT NULL,
    phone_number   VARCHAR2(1000) NOT NULL,
    CONSTRAINT employees_pk PRIMARY KEY (employee_id)
);
```

The database automatically creates an index for the primary key. That means there is an index on the EMPLOYEE_ID column, even though there is no **create index** statement.

The following query uses the primary key to retrieve an employee's name:

```
SELECT first_name, last_name
  FROM employees
 WHERE employee_id = 123
```

The **where** clause cannot match multiple rows because the primary key constraint ensures uniqueness of the EMPLOYEE_ID values. The database does not need to follow the index leaf nodes—it is enough to traverse the index tree. We can use the so-called *execution plan* for verification:

```
---------------------------------------------------------------
|Id |Operation                   | Name         | Rows | Cost |
---------------------------------------------------------------
| 0 |SELECT STATEMENT            |              |   1  |   2  |
| 1 | TABLE ACCESS BY INDEX ROWID| EMPLOYEES    |   1  |   2  |
|*2 |  INDEX UNIQUE SCAN         | EMPLOYEES_PK |   1  |   1  |
---------------------------------------------------------------

Predicate Information (identified by operation id):
---------------------------------------------------
   2 - access("EMPLOYEE_ID"=123)
```

The Oracle execution plan shows an INDEX UNIQUE SCAN—the operation that only traverses the index tree. It fully utilizes the logarithmic scalability of the index to find the entry very quickly—almost independent of the table size.

> **TIP**
>
> The *execution plan* (sometimes *explain plan* or *query plan*) shows the steps the database takes to execute an SQL statement. Appendix A on page 165 explains how to retrieve and read execution plans with other databases.

After accessing the index, the database must do one more step to fetch the queried data (FIRST_NAME, LAST_NAME) from the table storage: the TABLE ACCESS BY INDEX ROWID operation. This operation can become a performance bottleneck—as explained in "Slow Indexes, Part I"—but there is no such risk in connection with an INDEX UNIQUE SCAN. This operation cannot deliver more than one entry so it cannot trigger more than one table access. That means that the ingredients of a slow query are not present with an INDEX UNIQUE SCAN.

PRIMARY KEYS WITHOUT UNIQUE INDEX

A primary key does not necessarily need a unique index—you can use a non-unique index as well. In that case the Oracle database does not use an INDEX UNIQUE SCAN but instead the INDEX RANGE SCAN operation. Nonetheless, the constraint still maintains the uniqueness of keys so that the index lookup delivers at most one entry.

One of the reasons for using non-unique indexes for a primary keys are *deferrable constraints*. As opposed to regular constraints, which are validated during statement execution, the database postpones the validation of deferrable constraints until the transaction is committed. Deferred constraints are required for inserting data into tables with circular dependencies.

CONCATENATED INDEXES

Even though the database creates the index for the primary key automatically, there is still room for manual refinements if the key consists of multiple columns. In that case the database creates an index on all primary key columns—a so-called *concatenated* index (also known as *multi-column, composite* or *combined* index). Note that the column order of a concatenated index has great impact on its usability so it must be chosen carefully.

For the sake of demonstration, let's assume there is a company merger. The employees of the other company are added to our EMPLOYEES table so it becomes ten times as large. There is only one problem: the EMPLOYEE_ID is not unique across both companies. We need to extend the primary key by an extra identifier—e.g., a subsidiary ID. Thus the new primary key has two columns: the EMPLOYEE_ID as before and the SUBSIDIARY_ID to reestablish uniqueness.

The index for the new primary key is therefore defined in the following way:

```
CREATE UNIQUE INDEX employee_pk
    ON employees (employee_id, subsidiary_id);
```

A query for a particular employee has to take the full primary key into account—that is, the SUBSIDIARY_ID column also has to be used:

```
SELECT first_name, last_name
  FROM employees
 WHERE employee_id   = 123
   AND subsidiary_id = 30;

--------------------------------------------------------------
|Id |Operation                    | Name         | Rows | Cost |
--------------------------------------------------------------
| 0 |SELECT STATEMENT             |              |    1 |    2 |
| 1 | TABLE ACCESS BY INDEX ROWID| EMPLOYEES     |    1 |    2 |
|*2 |  INDEX UNIQUE SCAN          | EMPLOYEES_PK |    1 |    1 |
--------------------------------------------------------------

Predicate Information (identified by operation id):
--------------------------------------------------------
   2 - access("EMPLOYEE_ID"=123 AND "SUBSIDIARY_ID"=30)
```

CONCATENATED INDEXES

Whenever a query uses the complete primary key, the database can use
an INDEX UNIQUE SCAN—no matter how many columns the index has. But
what happens when using only one of the key columns, for example, when
searching all employees of a subsidiary?

```
SELECT first_name, last_name
  FROM employees
 WHERE subsidiary_id = 20;


---------------------------------------------------
| Id | Operation         | Name      | Rows | Cost |
---------------------------------------------------
|  0 | SELECT STATEMENT  |           |  106 |  478 |
|* 1 |  TABLE ACCESS FULL| EMPLOYEES |  106 |  478 |
---------------------------------------------------

Predicate Information (identified by operation id):
---------------------------------------------------
   1 - filter("SUBSIDIARY_ID"=20)
```

The execution plan reveals that the database does not use the index. Instead
it performs a FULL TABLE SCAN. As a result the database reads the entire table
and evaluates every row against the **where** clause. The execution time grows
with the table size: if the table grows tenfold, the FULL TABLE SCAN takes ten
times as long. The danger of this operation is that it is often fast enough
in a small development environment, but it causes serious performance
problems in production.

FULL TABLE SCAN

The operation TABLE ACCESS FULL, also known as *full table scan*, can
be the most efficient operation in some cases anyway, in particular
when retrieving a large part of the table.

This is partly due to the overhead for the index lookup itself, which
does not happen for a TABLE ACCESS FULL operation. This is mostly
because an index lookup reads one block after the other as the
database does not know which block to read next until the current
block has been processed. A FULL TABLE SCAN must get the entire table
anyway so that the database can read larger chunks at a time (*multi
block read*). Although the database reads more data, it might need to
execute fewer read operations.

13

CHAPTER 2: THE WHERE CLAUSE

The database does not use the index because it cannot use single columns from a concatenated index arbitrarily. A closer look at the index structure makes this clear.

A concatenated index is just a B-tree index like any other that keeps the indexed data in a sorted list. The database considers each column according to its position in the index definition to sort the index entries. The first column is the primary sort criterion and the second column determines the order only if two entries have the same value in the first column and so on.

> **IMPORTANT**
>
> A concatenated index is *one index across multiple columns*.

The ordering of a two-column index is therefore like the ordering of a telephone directory: it is first sorted by surname, then by first name. That means that a two-column index does not support searching on the second column alone; that would be like searching a telephone directory by first name.

Figure 2.1. Concatenated Index

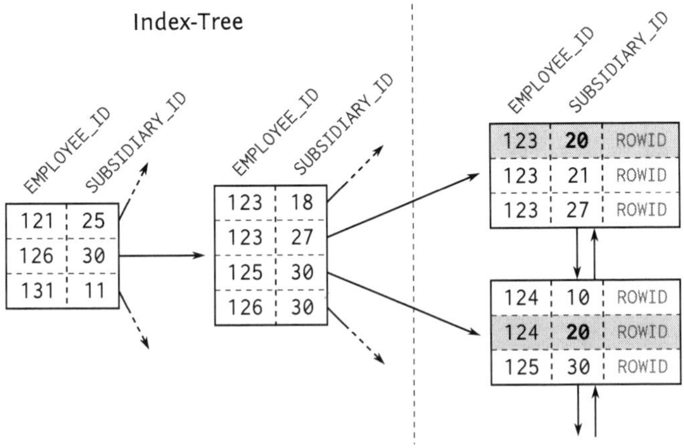

Index-Tree

The index excerpt in Figure 2.1 shows that the entries for subsidiary 20 are not stored next to each other. It is also apparent that there are no entries with SUBSIDIARY_ID = 20 in the tree, although they exist in the leaf nodes. The tree is therefore useless for this query.

14

CONCATENATED INDEXES

> **TIP**
>
> Visualizing an index helps in understanding what queries the index supports. You can query the database to retrieve the entries in index order (SQL:2008 syntax, see page 144 for proprietary solutions using LIMIT, TOP or ROWNUM):
>
> ```
> SELECT <INDEX COLUMN LIST>
>   FROM <TABLE>
>  ORDER BY <INDEX COLUMN LIST>
>  FETCH FIRST 100 ROWS ONLY;
> ```
>
> If you put the index definition and table name into the query, you will get a sample from the index. Ask yourself if the requested rows are clustered in a central place. If not, the index tree cannot help find that place.

We could, of course, add another index on SUBSIDIARY_ID to improve query speed. There is however a better solution—at least if we assume that searching on EMPLOYEE_ID alone does not make sense.

We can take advantage of the fact that the first index column is always usable for searching. Again, it is like a telephone directory: you don't need to know the first name to search by last name. The trick is to reverse the index column order so that the SUBSIDIARY_ID is in the first position:

```
CREATE UNIQUE INDEX EMPLOYEES_PK
    ON EMPLOYEES (SUBSIDIARY_ID, EMPLOYEE_ID);
```

Both columns together are still unique so queries with the full primary key can still use an INDEX UNIQUE SCAN but the sequence of index entries is entirely different. The SUBSIDIARY_ID has become the primary sort criterion. That means that all entries for a subsidiary are in the index consecutively so the database can use the B-tree to find their location.

15

CHAPTER 2: THE WHERE CLAUSE

> 💡 **IMPORTANT**
>
> The most important consideration when defining a concatenated index is how to choose the column order so it can be used as often as possible.

The execution plan confirms that the database uses the "reversed" index. The SUBSIDIARY_ID alone is not unique anymore so the database must follow the leaf nodes in order to find all matching entries: it is therefore using the INDEX RANGE SCAN operation.

```
---------------------------------------------------------------
|Id |Operation                 | Name        | Rows | Cost |
---------------------------------------------------------------
|  0 |SELECT STATEMENT          |             | 106 |   75 |
|  1 | TABLE ACCESS BY INDEX ROWID| EMPLOYEES  | 106 |   75 |
|*2 |  INDEX RANGE SCAN         | EMPLOYEE_PK | 106 |    2 |
---------------------------------------------------------------

Predicate Information (identified by operation id):
---------------------------------------------------
   2 - access("SUBSIDIARY_ID"=20)
```

In general, a database can use a concatenated index when searching with the leading (leftmost) columns. An index with three columns can be used when searching for the first column, when searching with the first two columns together, and when searching using all columns.

Even though the two-index solution delivers very good **select** performance as well, the single-index solution is preferable. It not only saves storage space, but also the maintenance overhead for the second index. The fewer indexes a table has, the better the **insert**, **delete** and **update** performance.

To define an optimal index you must understand more than just how indexes work—you must also know how the application queries the data. This means you have to know the column combinations that appear in the **where** clause.

Defining an optimal index is therefore very difficult for external consultants because they don't have an overview of the application's access paths. Consultants can usually consider one query only. They do not exploit the extra benefit the index could bring for other queries. Database administrators are in a similar position as they might know the database schema but do not have deep insight into the access paths.

16

CONCATENATED INDEXES

The only place where the technical database knowledge meets the functional knowledge of the business domain is the development department. Developers have a feeling for the data and know the access path. They can properly index to get the best benefit for the overall application without much effort.

CHAPTER 2: THE WHERE CLAUSE

SLOW INDEXES, PART II

The previous section explained how to gain additional benefits from an existing index by changing its column order, but the example considered only two SQL statements. Changing an index, however, may affect all queries on the indexed table. This section explains the way databases pick an index and demonstrates the possible side effects when changing existing indexes.

The adopted EMPLOYEE_PK index improves the performance of all queries that search by subsidiary only. It is however usable for all queries that search by SUBSIDIARY_ID—regardless of whether there are any additional search criteria. That means the index becomes usable for queries that used to use another index with another part of the **where** clause. In that case, if there are multiple access paths available it is the optimizer's job to choose the best one.

THE QUERY OPTIMIZER

The query optimizer, or query planner, is the database component that transforms an SQL statement into an execution plan. This process is also called *compiling* or *parsing*. There are two distinct optimizer types.

Cost-based optimizers (CBO) generate many execution plan variations and calculate a *cost* value for each plan. The cost calculation is based on the operations in use and the estimated row numbers. In the end the cost value serves as the benchmark for picking the "best" execution plan.

Rule-based optimizers (RBO) generate the execution plan using a hard-coded rule set. Rule based optimizers are less flexible and are seldom used today.

Changing an index might have unpleasant side effects as well. In our example, it is the internal telephone directory application that has become very slow since the merger. The first analysis identified the following query as the cause for the slowdown:

```
SELECT first_name, last_name, subsidiary_id, phone_number
  FROM employees
 WHERE last_name  = 'WINAND'
   AND subsidiary_id = 30;
```

The execution plan is:

Example 2.1. Execution Plan with Revised Primary Key Index

```
---------------------------------------------------------------
|Id |Operation                   | Name         | Rows | Cost |
---------------------------------------------------------------
| 0 |SELECT STATEMENT            |              |    1 |   30 |
|*1 | TABLE ACCESS BY INDEX ROWID| EMPLOYEES    |    1 |   30 |
|*2 |  INDEX RANGE SCAN          | EMPLOYEES_PK |   40 |    2 |
---------------------------------------------------------------

Predicate Information (identified by operation id):
--------------------------------------------------
  1 - filter("LAST_NAME"='WINAND')
  2 - access("SUBSIDIARY_ID"=30)
```

The execution plan uses an index and has an overall cost value of 30. So far, so good. It is however suspicious that it uses the index we just changed—that is enough reason to suspect that our index change caused the performance problem, especially when bearing the old index definition in mind—it started with the EMPLOYEE_ID column which is not part of the where clause at all. The query could not use that index before.

For further analysis, it would be nice to compare the execution plan before and after the change. To get the original execution plan, we could just deploy the old index definition again, however most databases offer a simpler method to prevent using an index for a specific query. The following example uses an Oracle *optimizer hint* for that purpose.

```
SELECT /*+ NO_INDEX(EMPLOYEES EMPLOYEE_PK) */
       first_name, last_name, subsidiary_id, phone_number
  FROM employees
 WHERE last_name  = 'WINAND'
   AND subsidiary_id = 30;
```

CHAPTER 2: THE WHERE CLAUSE

The execution plan that was presumably used before the index change did not use an index at all:

```
---------------------------------------------------------
| Id | Operation        | Name      | Rows | Cost |
---------------------------------------------------------
|  0 | SELECT STATEMENT |           |    1 |  477 |
|* 1 | TABLE ACCESS FULL| EMPLOYEES |    1 |  477 |
---------------------------------------------------------

Predicate Information (identified by operation id):
---------------------------------------------------------
   1 - filter("LAST_NAME"='WINAND' AND "SUBSIDIARY_ID"=30)
```

Even though the TABLE ACCESS FULL must read and process the entire table, it seems to be faster than using the index in this case. That is particularly unusual because the query matches one row only. Using an index to find a single row should be much faster than a full table scan, but in this case it is not. The index seems to be slow.

In such cases it is best to go through each step of the troublesome execution plan. The first step is the INDEX RANGE SCAN on the EMPLOYEES_PK index. That index does not cover the LAST_NAME column—the INDEX RANGE SCAN can consider the SUBSIDIARY_ID filter only; the Oracle database shows this in the "Predicate Information" area—entry "2" of the execution plan. There you can see the conditions that are applied for each operation.

> **TIP**
>
> Appendix A, *"Execution Plans"*, explains how to find the "Predicate Information" for other databases.

The INDEX RANGE SCAN with operation ID 2 (Example 2.1 on page 19) applies only the SUBSIDIARY_ID=30 filter. That means that it traverses the index tree to find the first entry for SUBSIDIARY_ID 30. Next it follows the leaf node chain to find all other entries for that subsidiary. The result of the INDEX RANGE SCAN is a list of ROWIDs that fulfill the SUBSIDIARY_ID condition: depending on the subsidiary size, there might be just a few ones or there could be many hundreds.

The next step is the TABLE ACCESS BY INDEX ROWID operation. It uses the ROWIDs from the previous step to fetch the rows—all columns—from the table. Once the LAST_NAME column is available, the database can evaluate the remaining part of the where clause. That means the database has to fetch all rows for SUBSIDIARY_ID=30 before it can apply the LAST_NAME filter.

The statement's response time does not depend on the result set size but on the number of employees in the particular subsidiary. If the subsidiary has just a few members, the INDEX RANGE SCAN provides better performance. Nonetheless a TABLE ACCESS FULL can be faster for a huge subsidiary because it can read large parts from the table in one shot (see "Full Table Scan" on page 13).

The query is slow because the index lookup returns many ROWIDs — one for each employee of the original company — and the database must fetch them individually. It is the perfect combination of the two ingredients that make an index slow: the database reads a wide index range and has to fetch many rows individually.

Choosing the best execution plan depends on the table's data distribution as well so the optimizer uses statistics about the contents of the database. In our example, a histogram containing the distribution of employees over subsidiaries is used. This allows the optimizer to estimate the number of rows returned from the index lookup — the result is used for the cost calculation.

STATISTICS

A cost-based optimizer uses statistics about tables, columns, and indexes. Most statistics are collected on the column level: the number of distinct values, the smallest and largest values (data range), the number of NULL occurrences and the column histogram (data distribution). The most important statistical value for a table is its size (in rows and blocks).

The most important index statistics are the tree depth, the number of leaf nodes, the number of distinct keys and the clustering factor (see Chapter 5, *Clustering Data*).

The optimizer uses these values to estimate the selectivity of the where clause predicates.

21

CHAPTER 2: THE WHERE CLAUSE

If there are no statistics available – for example because they were deleted – the optimizer uses default values. The default statistics of the Oracle database suggest a small index with medium selectivity. They lead to the estimate that the INDEX RANGE SCAN will return 40 rows. The execution plan shows this estimation in the Rows column (again, see Example 2.1 on page 19). Obviously this is a gross underestimate, as there are 1000 employees working for this subsidiary.

If we provide correct statistics, the optimizer does a better job. The following execution plan shows the new estimation: 1000 rows for the INDEX RANGE SCAN. Consequently it calculated a higher cost value for the subsequent table access.

```
----------------------------------------------------------------
|Id |Operation                   | Name        | Rows | Cost |
----------------------------------------------------------------
| 0 |SELECT STATEMENT            |             |    1 |  680 |
|*1 | TABLE ACCESS BY INDEX ROWID| EMPLOYEES   |    1 |  680 |
|*2 |  INDEX RANGE SCAN          | EMPLOYEES_PK | 1000 |    4 |
----------------------------------------------------------------

Predicate Information (identified by operation id):
---------------------------------------------------
  1 - filter("LAST_NAME"='WINAND')
  2 - access("SUBSIDIARY_ID"=30)
```

The cost value of 680 is even higher than the cost value for the execution plan using the FULL TABLE SCAN (477, see page 20). The optimizer will therefore automatically prefer the FULL TABLE SCAN.

This example of a slow index should not hide the fact that proper indexing is the best solution. Of course searching on last name is best supported by an index on LAST_NAME:

```
CREATE INDEX emp_name ON employees (last_name);
```

22

Slow Indexes, Part II

Using the new index, the optimizer calculates a cost value of 3:

Example 2.2. Execution Plan with Dedicated Index

```
---------------------------------------------------------------
| Id | Operation                   | Name      | Rows | Cost |
---------------------------------------------------------------
|  0 | SELECT STATEMENT            |           |   1  |   3  |
|* 1 |  TABLE ACCESS BY INDEX ROWID| EMPLOYEES |   1  |   3  |
|* 2 |    INDEX RANGE SCAN         | EMP_NAME  |   1  |   1  |
---------------------------------------------------------------

Predicate Information (identified by operation id):
---------------------------------------------------------
   1 - filter("SUBSIDIARY_ID"=30)
   2 - access("LAST_NAME"='WINAND')
```

The index access delivers—according to the optimizer's estimation—one row only. The database thus has to fetch only that row from the table: this is definitely faster than a FULL TABLE SCAN. A properly defined index is still better than the original full table scan.

The two execution plans from Example 2.1 (page 19) and Example 2.2 are almost identical. The database performs the same operations and the optimizer calculated similar cost values, nevertheless the second plan performs much better. The efficiency of an INDEX RANGE SCAN may vary over a wide range—especially when followed by a table access. Using an index does not automatically mean a statement is executed in the best way possible.

CHAPTER 2: THE WHERE CLAUSE

FUNCTIONS

The index on LAST_NAME has improved the performance considerably, but it requires you to search using the same case (upper/lower) as is stored in the database. This section explains how to lift this restriction without a decrease in performance.

> **NOTE**
>
> MySQL 5.6 does not support function-based indexing as described below. As an alternative, virtual columns were planned for MySQL 6.0 but were introduced in MariaDB 5.2 only.

CASE-INSENSITIVE SEARCH USING UPPER OR LOWER

Ignoring the case in a **where** clause is very simple. You can, for example, convert both sides of the comparison to all caps notation:

```
SELECT first_name, last_name, phone_number
  FROM employees
 WHERE UPPER(last_name) = UPPER('winand');
```

Regardless of the capitalization used for the search term or the LAST_NAME column, the UPPER function makes them match as desired.

> **NOTE**
>
> Another way for case-insensitive matching is to use a different "collation". The default collations used by SQL Server and MySQL do not distinguish between upper and lower case letters—they are case-insensitive by default.

24

The logic of this query is perfectly reasonable but the execution plan is not:

```
---------------------------------------------------------
| Id | Operation          | Name      | Rows | Cost |
---------------------------------------------------------
|  0 | SELECT STATEMENT   |           |   10 |  477 |
|* 1 |  TABLE ACCESS FULL | EMPLOYEES |   10 |  477 |
---------------------------------------------------------

Predicate Information (identified by operation id):
---------------------------------------------------------
   1 - filter(UPPER("LAST_NAME")='WINAND')
```

It is a return of our old friend the full table scan. Although there is an index on LAST_NAME, it is unusable—because the search is *not* on LAST_NAME but on UPPER(LAST_NAME). From the database's perspective, that's something *entirely different*.

This is a trap we all might fall into. We recognize the relation between LAST_NAME and UPPER(LAST_NAME) instantly and expect the database to "see" it as well. In reality the optimizer's view is more like this:

```
SELECT first_name, last_name, phone_number
  FROM employees
 WHERE BLACKBOX(...) = 'WINAND';
```

The UPPER function is just a black box. The parameters to the function are not relevant because there is no general relationship between the function's parameters and the result.

TIP

Replace the function name with BLACKBOX to understand the optimizer's point of view.

COMPILE TIME EVALUATION

The optimizer can evaluate the expression on the right-hand side during "compile time" because it has all the input parameters. The Oracle execution plan ("Predicate Information" section) therefore only shows the upper case notation of the search term. This behavior is very similar to a compiler that evaluates constant expressions at compile time.

CHAPTER 2: THE WHERE CLAUSE

To support that query, we need an index that covers the actual search term. That means we do not need an index on LAST_NAME but on UPPER(LAST_NAME):

```
CREATE INDEX emp_up_name
    ON employees (UPPER(last_name));
```

An index whose definition contains functions or expressions is a so-called *function-based index (FBI)*. Instead of copying the column data directly into the index, a function-based index applies the function first and puts the result into the index. As a result, the index stores the names in all caps notation.

The database can use a function-based index if the *exact* expression of the index definition appears in an SQL statement—like in the example above. The execution plan confirms this:

```
-----------------------------------------------------------
|Id |Operation                  | Name          | Rows | Cost |
-----------------------------------------------------------
| 0 |SELECT STATEMENT           |               | 100  |  41  |
| 1 | TABLE ACCESS BY INDEX ROWID| EMPLOYEES    | 100  |  41  |
|*2 |  INDEX RANGE SCAN          | EMP_UP_NAME   |  40  |   1  |
-----------------------------------------------------------

Predicate Information (identified by operation id):
---------------------------------------------------
   2 - access(UPPER("LAST_NAME")='WINAND')
```

It is a regular INDEX RANGE SCAN as described in Chapter 1. The database traverses the B-tree and follows the leaf node chain. There are no dedicated operations or keywords for function-based indexes.

> **WARNING**
>
> Sometimes ORM tools use UPPER and LOWER without the developer's knowledge. Hibernate, for example, injects an implicit LOWER for case-insensitive searches.

The execution plan is not yet the same as it was in the previous section without UPPER; the row count estimate is too high. It is particularly strange that the optimizer expects to fetch more rows from the table than the INDEX RANGE SCAN delivers in the first place. How can it fetch 100 rows from the table if the preceding index scan returned only 40 rows? The answer is that it can not. Contradicting estimates like this often indicate problems with the statistics. In this particular case it is because the Oracle database

26

CASE-INSENSITIVE SEARCH USING UPPER OR LOWER

does not update the table statistics when creating a new index (see also "Oracle Statistics for Function-Based Indexes" on page 28).

After updating the statistics, the optimizer calculates more accurate estimates:

```
--------------------------------------------------------------
|Id |Operation                     | Name        | Rows | Cost |
--------------------------------------------------------------
| 0 |SELECT STATEMENT              |             |   1  |   3  |
| 1 | TABLE ACCESS BY INDEX ROWID| EMPLOYEES    |   1  |   3  |
|*2 |  INDEX RANGE SCAN            | EMP_UP_NAME  |   1  |   1  |
--------------------------------------------------------------

Predicate Information (identified by operation id):
--------------------------------------------------------
  2 - access(UPPER("LAST_NAME")='WINAND')
```

> **NOTE**
>
> The so-called "extended statistics" on expressions and column groups were introduced with Oracle release 11g.

Although the updated statistics do not improve execution performance in this case—the index was properly used anyway—it is always a good idea to check the optimizer's estimates. The number of rows processed for each operation (cardinality estimate) is a particularly important figure that is also shown in SQL Server and PostgreSQL execution plans.

> **TIP**
>
> Appendix A, "*Execution Plans*", describes the row count estimates in SQL Server and PostgreSQL execution plans.

SQL Server does not support function-based indexes as described but it does offer computed columns that can be used instead. To make use of this, you have to first add a computed column to the table that can be indexed afterwards:

```
ALTER TABLE employees ADD last_name_up AS UPPER(last_name);
CREATE INDEX emp_up_name ON employees (last_name_up);
```

SQL Server is able to use this index whenever the indexed expression appears in the statement. In case of indexes just using a function like shown above, SQL Server can use the index automatically—it's not needed to

CHAPTER 2: THE WHERE CLAUSE

change the query. In other cases—like indexed expressions such as X + 1—you need to change the query to use the computed column in the **where** clause. Always check the execution plan in case of doubt.

ORACLE STATISTICS FOR FUNCTION-BASED INDEXES

The Oracle database maintains the information about the number of distinct column values as part of the table statistics. These figures are reused if a column is part of multiple indexes.

Statistics for a function-based index (FBI) are also kept on table level as *virtual columns*. Although the Oracle database collects the *index statistics* for new indexes automatically (since release 10g), it does not update the *table statistics*. For this reason, the Oracle documentation recommends updating the table statistics after creating a function-based index:

> After creating a function-based index, collect statistics on both the index and its base table using the DBMS_STATS package. Such statistics will enable Oracle Database to correctly decide when to use the index.
> —Oracle Database SQL Language Reference

My personal recommendation goes even further: after every index change, update the statistics for the base table and all its indexes. That might, however, also lead to unwanted side effects. Coordinate this activity with the database administrators (DBAs) and make a backup of the original statistics.

28

USER-DEFINED FUNCTIONS

Function-based indexing is a very generic approach. Besides functions like UPPER you can also index expressions like A + B and even use user-defined functions in the index definition.

There is one important exception. It is, for example, not possible to refer to the current time in an index definition, neither directly nor indirectly, as in the following example.

```
CREATE FUNCTION get_age(date_of_birth DATE)
RETURN NUMBER
AS
BEGIN
  RETURN
    TRUNC(MONTHS_BETWEEN(SYSDATE, date_of_birth)/12);
END;
/
```

The function GET_AGE uses the current date (SYSDATE) to calculate the age based on the supplied date of birth. You can use this function in all parts of an SQL query, for example in **select** and the **where** clauses:

```
SELECT first_name, last_name, get_age(date_of_birth)
  FROM employees
 WHERE get_age(date_of_birth) = 42;
```

The query lists all 42-year-old employees. Using a function-based index is an obvious idea for optimizing this query, but you cannot use the function GET_AGE in an index definition because it is not *deterministic*. That means the result of the function call is not fully determined by its parameters. Only functions that always return the same result for the same parameters— functions that are deterministic—can be indexed.

The reason behind this limitation is simple. When inserting a new row, the database calls the function and stores the result in the index and there it stays, unchanged. There is no periodic process that updates the index. The database updates the indexed age only when the date of birth is changed by an **update** statement. After the next birthday, the age that is stored in the index will be wrong.

29

CHAPTER 2: THE WHERE CLAUSE

Besides *being* deterministic, PostgreSQL and the Oracle database require functions to be *declared* to be deterministic when used in an index so you have to use the keyword DETERMINISTIC (Oracle) or IMMUTABLE (PostgreSQL).

> **CAUTION**
>
> PostgreSQL and the Oracle database trust the DETERMINISTIC or IMMUTABLE declarations—that means they trust the developer.
>
> You can declare the GET_AGE function to be deterministic and use it in an index definition. Regardless of the declaration, it will *not* work as intended because the age stored in the index will not increase as the years pass; the employees will not get older—at least not in the index.

Other examples for functions that cannot be "indexed" are random number generators and functions that depend on environment variables.

> **THINK ABOUT IT**
>
> How can you still use an index to optimize a query for all 42-year-old employees?

Over-Indexing

If the concept of function-based indexing is new to you, you might be tempted to just index everything, but this is in fact the very last thing you should do. The reason is that every index causes ongoing maintenance. Function-based indexes are particularly troublesome because they make it very easy to create *redundant indexes*.

The case-insensitive search from above could be implemented with the LOWER function as well:

```
SELECT first_name, last_name, phone_number
  FROM employees
 WHERE LOWER(last_name) = LOWER('winand');
```

A single index cannot support both methods of ignoring the case. We could, of course, create a second index on LOWER(last_name) for this query, but that would mean the database has to maintain two indexes for each **insert**, **update**, and **delete** statement (see also Chapter 8, *"Modifying Data"*). To make one index suffice, you should consistently use the same function throughout your application.

> **TIP**
>
> Unify the access path so that one index can be used by several queries.

> **TIP**
>
> Always aim to index the original data as that is often the most useful information you can put into an index.

Parameterized Queries

This section covers a topic that is skipped in most SQL textbooks: *parameterized queries* and *bind parameters*.

Bind parameters—also called dynamic parameters or bind variables—are an alternative way to pass data to the database. Instead of putting the values directly into the SQL statement, you just use a placeholder like ?, :name or @name and provide the actual values using a separate API call.

There is nothing bad about writing values directly into ad-hoc statements; there are, however, two good reasons to use bind parameters in programs:

SECURITY
> Bind variables are the best way to prevent SQL injection[1].

PERFORMANCE
> Databases with an execution plan cache like SQL Server and the Oracle database can reuse an execution plan when executing the same statement multiple times. It saves effort in rebuilding the execution plan but works only if the SQL statement is *exactly* the same. If you put different values into the SQL statement, the database handles it like a different statement and recreates the execution plan.

When using bind parameters you do not write the actual values but instead insert placeholders into the SQL statement. That way the statements do not change when executing them with different values.

---

[1] http://en.wikipedia.org/wiki/SQL_injection

PARAMETERIZED QUERIES

Naturally there are exceptions, for example if the affected data volume depends on the actual values:

```
99 rows selected.

SELECT first_name, last_name
  FROM employees
 WHERE subsidiary_id = 20;
```

```
--------------------------------------------------------------
|Id | Operation                  | Name        | Rows | Cost |
--------------------------------------------------------------
| 0 | SELECT STATEMENT           |             |   99 |   70 |
| 1 |  TABLE ACCESS BY INDEX ROWID| EMPLOYEES   |   99 |   70 |
|*2 |   INDEX RANGE SCAN         | EMPLOYEE_PK |   99 |    2 |
--------------------------------------------------------------

Predicate Information (identified by operation id):
---------------------------------------------------

   2 - access("SUBSIDIARY_ID"=20)
```

An index lookup delivers the best performance for small subsidiaries, but a TABLE ACCESS FULL can outperform the index for large subsidiaries:

```
1000 rows selected.

SELECT first_name, last_name
  FROM employees
 WHERE subsidiary_id = 30;
```

```
------------------------------------------------------
| Id | Operation        | Name      | Rows | Cost |
------------------------------------------------------
|  0 | SELECT STATEMENT |           | 1000 |  478 |
|* 1 |  TABLE ACCESS FULL| EMPLOYEES | 1000 |  478 |
------------------------------------------------------

Predicate Information (identified by operation id):
---------------------------------------------------

   1 - filter("SUBSIDIARY_ID"=30)
```

In this case, the histogram on SUBSIDIARY_ID fulfills its purpose. The optimizer uses it to determine the frequency of the subsidiary ID mentioned in the SQL query. Consequently it gets two different row count estimates for both queries.

33

CHAPTER 2: THE WHERE CLAUSE

The subsequent cost calculation will therefore result in two different cost values. When the optimizer finally selects an execution plan it takes the plan with the lowest cost value. For the smaller subsidiary, it is the one using the index.

The cost of the TABLE ACCESS BY INDEX ROWID operation is highly sensitive to the row count estimate. Selecting ten times as many rows will elevate the cost value by that factor. The overall cost using the index is then even higher than a full table scan. The optimizer will therefore select the other execution plan for the bigger subsidiary.

When using bind parameters, the optimizer has no concrete values available to determine their frequency. It then just assumes an equal distribution and always gets the same row count estimates and cost values. In the end, it will always select the same execution plan.

> **TIP**
>
> Column histograms are most useful if the values are not uniformly distributed.
>
> For columns with uniform distribution, it is often sufficient to divide the number of distinct values by the number of rows in the table. This method also works when using bind parameters.

If we compare the optimizer to a compiler, bind variables are like program variables, but if you write the values directly into the statement they are more like constants. The database can use the values from the SQL statement during optimization just like a compiler can evaluate constant expressions during compilation. Bind parameters are, put simply, not visible to the optimizer just as the runtime values of variables are not known to the compiler.

From this perspective, it is a little bit paradoxical that bind parameters can improve performance if not using bind parameters enables the optimizer to always opt for the best execution plan. But the question is at what price? Generating and evaluating all execution plan variants is a huge effort that does not pay off if you get the same result in the end anyway.

34

> **TIP**
>
> Not using bind parameters is like recompiling a program every time.

Deciding to build a specialized or generic execution plan presents a dilemma for the database. Either effort is taken to evaluate all possible plan variants for each execution in order to always get the best execution plan or the optimization overhead is saved and a cached execution plan is used whenever possible—accepting the risk of using a suboptimal execution plan. The quandary is that the database does not know if the full optimization cycle delivers a different execution plan without actually doing the full optimization. Database vendors try to solve this dilemma with heuristic methods—but with very limited success.

As the developer, you can use bind parameters deliberately to help resolve this dilemma. That is, you should always use bind parameters except for values that *shall* influence the execution plan.

Unevenly distributed status codes like "todo" and "done" are a good example. The number of "done" entries often exceeds the "todo" records by an order of magnitude. Using an index only makes sense when searching for "todo" entries in that case. Partitioning is another example—that is, if you split tables and indexes across several storage areas. The actual values can then influence which partitions have to be scanned. The performance of LIKE queries can suffer from bind parameters as well as we will see in the next section.

> **TIP**
>
> In all reality, there are only a few cases in which the actual values affect the execution plan. You should therefore use bind parameters if in doubt—just to prevent SQL injections.

The following code snippets show how to use bind parameters in various programming languages.

CHAPTER 2: THE WHERE CLAUSE

C#

Without bind parameters:

```
int subsidiary_id;
SqlCommand cmd = new SqlCommand(
                "select first_name, last_name"
          + "  from employees"
          + " where subsidiary_id = " + subsidiary_id
          , connection);
```

Using a bind parameter:

```
int subsidiary_id;
SqlCommand cmd =
       new SqlCommand(
                "select first_name, last_name"
          + "  from employees"
          + " where subsidiary_id = @subsidiary_id
          , connection);
cmd.Parameters.AddWithValue("@subsidiary_id", subsidiary_id);
```

See also: SqlParameterCollection class documentation.

JAVA

Without bind parameters:

```
int subsidiary_id;
Statement command = connection.createStatement(
                "select first_name, last_name"
          + "  from employees"
          + " where subsidiary_id = " + subsidiary_id
          );
```

Using a bind parameter:

```
int subsidiary_id;
PreparedStatement command = connection.prepareStatement(
                "select first_name, last_name"
          + "  from employees"
          + " where subsidiary_id = ?"
          );
command.setInt(1, subsidiary_id);
```

See also: PreparedStatement class documentation.

36

PARAMETERIZED QUERIES

PERL

Without bind parameters:

```
my $subsidiary_id;
my $sth = $dbh->prepare(
                  "select first_name, last_name"
           .  "  from employees"
           .  " where subsidiary_id = $subsidiary_id"
                  );
$sth->execute();
```

Using a bind parameter:

```
my $subsidiary_id;
my $sth = $dbh->prepare(
                  "select first_name, last_name"
           .  "  from employees"
           .  " where subsidiary_id = ?"
                  );
$sth->execute($subsidiary_id);
```

See: Programming the Perl DBI.

PHP

Using MySQL, without bind parameters:

```
$mysqli->query("select first_name, last_name"
          .  "  from employees"
          .  " where subsidiary_id = " . $subsidiary_id);
```

Using a bind parameter:

```
if ($stmt = $mysqli->prepare("select first_name, last_name"
                        .  "  from employees"
                        .  " where subsidiary_id = ?"))
{
   $stmt->bind_param("i", $subsidiary_id);
   $stmt->execute();
} else {
   /* handle SQL error */
}
```

See also: mysqli_stmt::bind_param class documentation and "Prepared statements and stored procedures" in the PDO documentation.

CHAPTER 2: THE WHERE CLAUSE

RUBY

Without bind parameters:

```
dbh.execute("select first_name, last_name"
          + "  from employees"
          + " where subsidiary_id = #{subsidiary_id}");
```

Using a bind parameter:

```
dbh.prepare("select first_name, last_name"
          + "  from employees"
          + " where subsidiary_id = ?");
dbh.execute(subsidiary_id);
```

See also: "Quoting, Placeholders, and Parameter Binding" in the Ruby DBI Tutorial.

The question mark (?) is the only placeholder character that the SQL standard defines. Question marks are positional parameters. That means the question marks are numbered from left to right. To bind a value to a particular question mark, you have to specify its number. That can, however, be very impractical because the numbering changes when adding or removing placeholders. Many databases offer a proprietary extension for named parameters to solve this problem—e.g., using an "at" symbol (@name) or a colon (:name).

> **NOTE**
>
> Bind parameters cannot change the structure of an SQL statement.
>
> That means you cannot use bind parameters for table or column names. The following bind parameters do not work:
>
> ```
> String sql = prepare("SELECT * FROM ? WHERE ?");
>
> sql.execute('employees', 'employee_id = 1');
> ```
>
> If you need to change the structure of an SQL statement during runtime, use dynamic SQL.

38

Cursor Sharing and Auto Parameterization

The more complex the optimizer and the SQL query become, the more important execution plan caching becomes. The SQL Server and Oracle databases have features to automatically replace the literal values in a SQL string with bind parameters. These features are called CURSOR_SHARING (Oracle) or *forced parameterization* (SQL Server).

Both features are workarounds for applications that do not use bind parameters at all. Enabling these features prevents developers from intentionally using literal values.

Searching for Ranges

Inequality operators such as <, > and **between** can use indexes just like the equals operator explained above. Even a LIKE filter can—under certain circumstances—use an index just like range conditions do.

Using these operations limits the choice of the column order in multi-column indexes. This limitation can even rule out all optimal indexing options—there are queries where you simply cannot define a "correct" column order at all.

Greater, Less and BETWEEN

The biggest performance risk of an INDEX RANGE SCAN is the leaf node traversal. It is therefore the golden rule of indexing to keep the scanned index range as small as possible. You can check that by asking yourself where an index scan starts and where it ends.

CHAPTER 2: THE WHERE CLAUSE

The question is easy to answer if the SQL statement mentions the start and stop conditions explicitly:

```
SELECT first_name, last_name, date_of_birth
  FROM employees
 WHERE date_of_birth >= TO_DATE(?, 'YYYY-MM-DD')
   AND date_of_birth <= TO_DATE(?, 'YYYY-MM-DD')
```

An index on DATE_OF_BIRTH is only scanned in the specified range. The scan starts at the first date and ends at the second. We cannot narrow the scanned index range any further.

The start and stop conditions are less obvious if a second column becomes involved:

```
SELECT first_name, last_name, date_of_birth
  FROM employees
 WHERE date_of_birth >= TO_DATE(?, 'YYYY-MM-DD')
   AND date_of_birth <= TO_DATE(?, 'YYYY-MM-DD')
   AND subsidiary_id  = ?
```

Of course an ideal index has to cover both columns, but the question is in which order?

The following figures show the effect of the column order on the scanned index range. For this illustration we search all employees of subsidiary 27 who were born between January 1st and January 9th 1971.

Figure 2.2 visualizes a detail of the index on DATE_OF_BIRTH and SUBSIDIARY_ID—in that order. Where will the database start to follow the leaf node chain, or to put it another way: where will the tree traversal end?

The index is ordered by birth dates first. Only if two employees were born on the same day is the SUBSIDIARY_ID used to sort these records. The query, however, covers a date *range*. The ordering of SUBSIDIARY_ID is therefore useless during tree traversal. That becomes obvious if you realize that there is no entry for subsidiary 27 in the branch nodes—although there is one in the leaf nodes. The filter on DATE_OF_BIRTH is therefore the only condition that limits the scanned index range. It starts at the first entry matching the date range and ends at the last one—all five leaf nodes shown in Figure 2.2.

40

GREATER, LESS AND BETWEEN

Figure 2.2. Range Scan in DATE_OF_BIRTH, SUBSIDIARY_ID **Index**

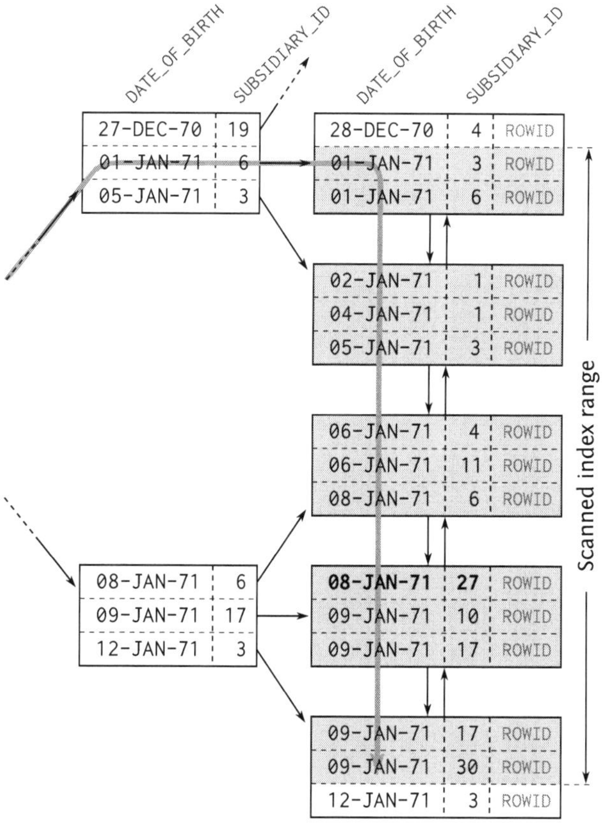

The picture looks entirely different when reversing the column order. Figure 2.3 illustrates the scan if the index starts with the SUBSIDIARY_ID column.

The difference is that the equals operator limits the first index column to a single value. Within the range for this value (SUBSIDIARY_ID 27) the index is sorted according to the second column—the date of birth—so there is no need to visit the first leaf node because the branch node already indicates that there is no employee for subsidiary 27 born after June 25th 1969 in the first leaf node.

41

CHAPTER 2: THE WHERE CLAUSE

Figure 2.3. Range Scan in SUBSIDIARY_ID, DATE_OF_BIRTH **Index**

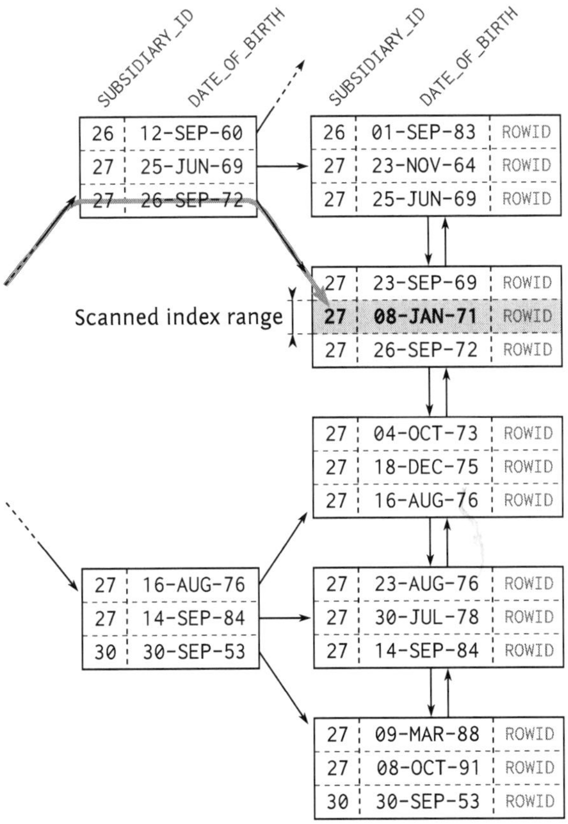

The tree traversal directly leads to the second leaf node. In this case, all **where** clause conditions limit the scanned index range so that the scan terminates at the very same leaf node.

> **TIP**
>
> Rule of thumb: index for equality first—then for ranges.

The actual performance difference depends on the data and search criteria. The difference can be negligible if the filter on DATE_OF_BIRTH is very selective on its own. The bigger the date range becomes, the bigger the performance difference will be.

42

GREATER, LESS AND BETWEEN

With this example, we can also falsify the myth that the most selective column should be at the leftmost index position. If we look at the figures and consider the selectivity of the first column only, we see that both conditions match 13 records. This is the case regardless whether we filter by DATE_OF_BIRTH only or by SUBSIDIARY_ID only. The selectivity is of no use here, but one column order is still better than the other.

To optimize performance, it is very important to know the scanned index range. With most databases you can even see this in the execution plan — you just have to know what to look for. The following execution plan from the Oracle database unambiguously indicates that the EMP_TEST index starts with the DATE_OF_BIRTH column.

```
---------------------------------------------------------------
|Id | Operation                      | Name      | Rows | Cost |
---------------------------------------------------------------
| 0 | SELECT STATEMENT               |           |   1  |   4  |
|*1 |  FILTER                        |           |      |      |
| 2 |   TABLE ACCESS BY INDEX ROWID| EMPLOYEES |   1  |   4  |
|*3 |    INDEX RANGE SCAN            | EMP_TEST  |   2  |   2  |
---------------------------------------------------------------

Predicate Information (identified by operation id):
---------------------------------------------------
1 - filter(:END_DT >= :START_DT)
3 - access(DATE_OF_BIRTH >= :START_DT
      AND DATE_OF_BIRTH <= :END_DT)
    filter(SUBSIDIARY_ID  = :SUBS_ID)
```

The *predicate information* for the INDEX RANGE SCAN gives the crucial hint. It identifies the conditions of the **where** clause either as *access* or as *filter* predicates. This is how the database tells us how it uses each condition.

NOTE

The execution plan was simplified for clarity. The appendix on page 170 explains the details of the "Predicate Information" section in an Oracle execution plan.

The conditions on the DATE_OF_BIRTH column are the only ones listed as access predicates; they limit the scanned index range. The DATE_OF_BIRTH is therefore the first column in the EMP_TEST index. The SUBSIDIARY_ID column is used only as a filter.

CHAPTER 2: THE WHERE CLAUSE

> **IMPORTANT**
>
> The *access predicates* are the start and stop conditions for an index lookup. They define the scanned index range.
>
> *Index filter predicates* are applied during the leaf node traversal only. They do not narrow the scanned index range.
>
> Appendix A explains how to recognize access predicates in other databases.

The database can use all conditions as access predicates if we turn the index definition around:

```
---------------------------------------------------------------
| Id | Operation                    | Name      | Rows | Cost |
---------------------------------------------------------------
|  0 | SELECT STATEMENT             |           |   1  |   3  |
|* 1 |  FILTER                      |           |      |      |
|  2 |   TABLE ACCESS BY INDEX ROWID| EMPLOYEES |   1  |   3  |
|* 3 |    INDEX RANGE SCAN          | EMP_TEST2 |   1  |   2  |
---------------------------------------------------------------

Predicate Information (identified by operation id):
---------------------------------------------------
1 - filter(:END_DT >= :START_DT)
3 - access(SUBSIDIARY_ID  = :SUBS_ID
       AND DATE_OF_BIRTH >= :START_DT
       AND DATE_OF_BIRTH <= :END_T)
```

Finally, there is the **between** operator. It allows you to specify the upper and lower bounds in a single condition:

```
DATE_OF_BIRTH BETWEEN '01-JAN-71'
                  AND '10-JAN-71'
```

Note that **between** always includes the specified values, just like using the less than or equal to (<=) and greater than or equal to (>=) operators:

```
    DATE_OF_BIRTH >= '01-JAN-71'
AND DATE_OF_BIRTH <= '10-JAN-71'
```

44

INDEXING LIKE FILTERS

The SQL LIKE operator very often causes unexpected performance behavior because some search terms prevent efficient index usage. That means that there are search terms that can be indexed very well, but others can not. It is the position of the wildcard characters that makes all the difference.

The following example uses the % wildcard in the middle of the search term:

```
SELECT first_name, last_name, date_of_birth
  FROM employees
 WHERE UPPER(last_name) LIKE 'WIN%D'
```

```
---------------------------------------------------------------
|Id | Operation                  | Name         | Rows | Cost |
---------------------------------------------------------------
| 0 | SELECT STATEMENT           |              |   1  |   4  |
| 1 |  TABLE ACCESS BY INDEX ROWID| EMPLOYEES   |   1  |   4  |
|*2 |   INDEX RANGE SCAN          | EMP_UP_NAME |   1  |   2  |
---------------------------------------------------------------
```

LIKE filters can only use the characters *before the first wildcard* during tree traversal. The remaining characters are just filter predicates that do not narrow the scanned index range. A single LIKE expression can therefore contain two predicate types: (1) the part before the first wildcard as an access predicate; (2) the other characters as a filter predicate.

> **CAUTION**
>
> For the PostgreSQL database, you might need to specify an operator class (e.g., `varchar_pattern_ops`) to use LIKE expressions as access predicates. Refer to "Operator Classes and Operator Families" in the PostgreSQL documentation for further details.

The more selective the prefix before the first wildcard is, the smaller the scanned index range becomes. That, in turn, makes the index lookup faster. Figure 2.4 illustrates this relationship using three different LIKE expressions. All three select the same row, but the scanned index range — and thus the performance — is very different.

CHAPTER 2: THE WHERE CLAUSE

Figure 2.4. Various LIKE **Searches**

LIKE 'WI%ND'	LIKE 'WIN%D'	LIKE 'WINA%'
WIAW	WIAW	WIAW
WIBLQQNPUA	WIBLQQNPUA	WIBLQQNPUA
WIBYHSNZ	WIBYHSNZ	WIBYHSNZ
WIFMDWUQMB	WIFMDWUQMB	WIFMDWUQMB
WIGLZX	WIGLZX	WIGLZX
WIH	WIH	WIH
WIHTFVZNLC	WIHTFVZNLC	WIHTFVZNLC
WIJYAXPP	WIJYAXPP	WIJYAXPP
WINAND	**WIN**AND	**WIN**AND
WINBKYDSKW	**WIN**BKYDSKW	WINBKYDSKW
WIPOJ	WIPOJ	WIPOJ
WISRGPK	WISRGPK	WISRGPK
WITJIVQJ	WITJIVQJ	WITJIVQJ
WIW	WIW	WIW
WIWGPJMQGG	WIWGPJMQGG	WIWGPJMQGG
WIWKHLBJ	WIWKHLBJ	WIWKHLBJ
WIYETHN	WIYETHN	WIYETHN
WIYJ	WIYJ	WIYJ

The first expression has two characters before the wildcard. They limit the scanned index range to 18 rows. Only one of them matches the entire LIKE expression—the other 17 are fetched but discarded. The second expression has a longer prefix that narrows the scanned index range down to two rows. With this expression, the database just reads one extra row that is not relevant for the result. The last expression does not have a filter predicate at all: the database just reads the entry that matches the entire LIKE expression.

IMPORTANT

Only the part before the first wildcard serves as an access predicate.

The remaining characters do not narrow the scanned index range—non-matching entries are just left out of the result.

The opposite case is also possible: a LIKE expression that starts with a wildcard. Such a LIKE expression cannot serve as an access predicate. The database has to scan the entire table if there are no other conditions that provide access predicates.

INDEXING LIKE FILTERS

> **TIP**
>
> Avoid LIKE expressions with leading wildcards (e.g., '%TERM').

The position of the wildcard characters affects index usage—at least in theory. In reality the optimizer creates a generic execution plan when the search term is supplied via bind parameters. In that case, the optimizer has to guess whether or not the majority of executions will have a leading wildcard.

Most databases just assume that there is no leading wildcard when optimizing a LIKE condition with bind parameter, but this assumption is wrong if the LIKE expression is used for a full-text search. There is, unfortunately, no direct way to tag a LIKE condition as full-text search. The box "Labeling Full-Text LIKE Expressions" shows an attempt that does not work. Specifying the search term without bind parameter is the most obvious solution, but that increases the optimization overhead and opens an SQL injection vulnerability. An effective but still secure and portable solution is to intentionally obfuscate the LIKE condition. "Combining Columns" on page 70 explains this in detail.

LABELING FULL-TEXT LIKE EXPRESSIONS

When using the LIKE operator for a full-text search, we could separate the wildcards from the search term:

```
WHERE text_column LIKE '%' || ? || '%'
```

The wildcards are directly written into the SQL statement, but we use a bind parameter for the search term. The final LIKE expression is built by the database itself using the string concatenation operator || (Oracle, PostgreSQL). Although using a bind parameter, the final LIKE expression will always start with a wildcard. Unfortunately databases do not recognize that.

For the PostgreSQL database, the problem is different because PostgreSQL assumes there *is* a leading wildcard when using bind parameters for a LIKE expression. PostgreSQL just does not use an index in that case. The only way to get an index access for a LIKE expression is to make the actual

47

CHAPTER 2: THE WHERE CLAUSE

search term visible to the optimizer. If you do not use a bind parameter but put the search term directly into the SQL statement, you must take other precautions against SQL injection attacks!

Even if the database optimizes the execution plan for a leading wildcard, it can still deliver insufficient performance. You can use another part of the **where** clause to access the data efficiently in that case—see also "Index Filter Predicates Used Intentionally" on page 112. If there is no other access path, you might use one of the following proprietary full-text index solutions.

MYSQL

MySQL offers the **match** and **against** keywords for full-text searching. Starting with MySQL 5.6, you can create full-text indexes for InnoDB tables as well—previously, this was only possible with MyISAM tables. See "Full-Text Search Functions" in the MySQL documentation.

ORACLE DATABASE

The Oracle database offers the **contains** keyword. See the "Oracle Text Application Developer's Guide."

POSTGRESQL

PostgreSQL offers the **@@** operator to implement full-text searches. See "Full Text Search" in the PostgreSQL documentation.

Another option is to use the WildSpeed[2] extension to optimize LIKE expressions directly. The extension stores the text in all possible rotations so that each character is at the beginning once. That means that the indexed text is not only stored once but instead as many times as there are characters in the string—thus it needs a lot of space.

SQL SERVER

SQL Server offers the **contains** keyword. See "Full-Text Search" in the SQL Server documentation.

THINK ABOUT IT

How can you index a LIKE search that has only one wildcard at the beginning of the search term ('%TERM')?

---

[2] http://www.sai.msu.su/~megera/wiki/wildspeed

48

Index Merge

It is one of the most common question about indexing: is it better to create one index for each column or a single index for all columns of a **where** clause? The answer is very simple in most cases: one index with multiple columns is better.

Nevertheless there are queries where a single index cannot do a perfect job, no matter how you define the index; e.g., queries with two or more independent range conditions as in the following example:

```
SELECT first_name, last_name, date_of_birth
  FROM employees
 WHERE UPPER(last_name) < ?
   AND date_of_birth   < ?
```

It is impossible to define a B-tree index that would support this query without filter predicates. For an explanation, you just need to remember that an index is a linked list.

If you define the index as UPPER(LAST_NAME), DATE_OF_BIRTH (in that order), the list begins with A and ends with Z. The date of birth is considered only when there are two employees with the same name. If you define the index the other way around, it will start with the eldest employees and end with the youngest. In that case, the names only have a minor impact on the sort order.

No matter how you twist and turn the index definition, the entries are always arranged along a chain. At one end, you have the small entries and at the other end the big ones. An index can therefore only support one range condition as an access predicate. Supporting two independent range conditions requires a second axis, for example like a chessboard. The query above would then match all entries from one corner of the chessboard, but an index is not like a chessboard—it is like a chain. There is no corner.

You can of course accept the filter predicate and use a multi-column index nevertheless. That is the best solution in many cases anyway. The index definition should then mention the more selective column first so it can be used with an access predicate. That might be the origin of the "most selective first" myth but this rule only holds true if you cannot avoid a filter predicate.

CHAPTER 2: THE WHERE CLAUSE

The other option is to use two separate indexes, one for each column. Then the database must scan both indexes first and then combine the results. The duplicate index lookup alone already involves more effort because the database has to traverse two index trees. Additionally, the database needs a lot of memory and CPU time to combine the intermediate results.

> **NOTE**
>
> One index scan is faster than two.

Databases use two methods to combine indexes. Firstly there is the index join. Chapter 4, "The Join Operation" explains the related algorithms in detail. The second approach makes use of functionality from the data warehouse world.

The data warehouse is the mother of all ad-hoc queries. It just needs a few clicks to combine arbitrary conditions into the query of your choice. It is impossible to predict the column combinations that might appear in the **where** clause and that makes indexing, as explained so far, almost impossible.

Data warehouses use a special purpose index type to solve that problem: the so-called *bitmap index*. The advantage of bitmap indexes is that they can be combined rather easily. That means you get decent performance when indexing each column individually. Conversely if you know the query in advance, so that you can create a tailored multi-column B-tree index, it will still be faster than combining multiple bitmap indexes.

By far the greatest weakness of bitmap indexes is the ridiculous **insert**, **update** and **delete** scalability. Concurrent write operations are virtually impossible. That is no problem in a data warehouse because the load processes are scheduled one after another. In online applications, bitmap indexes are mostly useless.

> **IMPORTANT**
>
> Bitmap indexes are almost unusable for online transaction processing (OLTP).

Many database products offer a hybrid solution between B-tree and bitmap indexes. In the absence of a better access path, they convert the results of several B-tree scans into in-memory bitmap structures. Those can be combined efficiently. The bitmap structures are not stored persistently but discarded after statement execution, thus bypassing the problem of the poor write scalability. The downside is that it needs a lot of memory and CPU time. This method is, after all, an optimizer's act of desperation.

PARTIAL INDEXES

So far we have only discussed which *columns* to add to an index. With *partial* (PostgreSQL) or *filtered* (SQL Server) indexes you can also specify the *rows* that are indexed.

> ### CAUTION
>
> The Oracle database has a unique approach to partial indexing. The next section explains it while building upon this section.

A partial index is useful for commonly used **where** conditions that use constant values—like the status code in the following example:

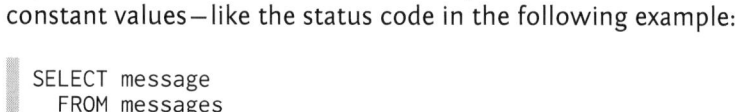

```
SELECT message
  FROM messages
 WHERE processed = 'N'
   AND receiver  = ?
```

Queries like this are very common in queuing systems. The query fetches all unprocessed messages for a specific recipient. Messages that were already processed are rarely needed. If they are needed, they are usually accessed by a more specific criteria like the primary key.

We can optimize this query with a two-column index. Considering this query only, the column order does not matter because there is no range condition.

```
CREATE INDEX messages_todo
          ON messages (receiver, processed)
```

The index fulfills its purpose, but it includes many rows that are never searched, namely all the messages that were already processed. Due to the logarithmic scalability the index nevertheless makes the query very fast even though it wastes a lot of disk space.

51

CHAPTER 2: THE WHERE CLAUSE

With partial indexing you can limit the index to include only the unprocessed messages. The syntax for this is surprisingly simple: a **where** clause.

```
CREATE INDEX messages_todo
        ON messages (receiver)
     WHERE processed = 'N'
```

The index only contains the rows that satisfy the **where** clause. In this particular case, we can even remove the PROCESSED column because it is always 'N' anyway. That means the index reduces its size in two dimensions: vertically, because it contains fewer rows; horizontally, due to the removed column.

The index is therefore very small. For a queue, it can even mean that the index size remains unchanged although the table grows without bounds. The index does not contain all messages, just the unprocessed ones.

The **where** clause of a partial index can become arbitrarily complex. The only fundamental limitation is about functions: you can only use deterministic functions as is the case everywhere in an index definition. SQL Server has, however, more restrictive rules and neither allow functions nor the OR operator in index predicates.

A database can use a partial index whenever the **where** clause appears in a query.

THINK ABOUT IT

What peculiarity has the smallest possible index for the following query:

```
SELECT message
  FROM messages
 WHERE processed = 'N';
```

52

NULL IN THE ORACLE DATABASE

SQL's NULL frequently causes confusion. Although the basic idea of NULL—to represent missing data—is rather simple, there are some peculiarities. You have to use IS NULL instead of = NULL, for example. Moreover the Oracle database has additional NULL oddities, on the one hand because it does not always handle NULL as required by the standard and on the other hand because it has a very "special" handling of NULL in indexes.

The SQL standard does not define NULL as a value but rather as a placeholder for a missing or unknown value. Consequently, no value can be NULL. Instead the Oracle database treats an empty string as NULL:

```
    SELECT     '0 IS NULL???' AS "what is NULL?" FROM dual
     WHERE     0 IS NULL
UNION ALL
    SELECT     '0 is not null' FROM dual
     WHERE     0 IS NOT NULL
UNION ALL
    SELECT '''''  IS NULL???'  FROM dual
     WHERE     '' IS NULL
UNION ALL
    SELECT '''''  is not null' FROM dual
     WHERE     '' IS NOT NULL;

what is NULL?
--------------
0 is not null
'' IS NULL???
```

To add to the confusion, there is even a case when the Oracle database treats NULL as empty string:

```
SELECT dummy
     , dummy || ''
     , dummy || NULL
  FROM dual;

D D D
- - -
X X X
```

Concatenating the DUMMY column (always containing 'X') with NULL should return NULL.

CHAPTER 2: THE WHERE CLAUSE

The concept of NULL is used in many programming languages. No matter where you look, an empty string is never NULL...except in the Oracle database. It is, in fact, impossible to store an empty string in a VARCHAR2 field. If you try, the Oracle database just stores NULL.

This peculiarity is not only strange; it is also dangerous. Additionally the Oracle database's NULL oddity does not stop here—it continues with indexing.

INDEXING NULL

The Oracle database does not include rows in an index if all indexed columns are NULL. That means that every index is a partial index—like having a **where** clause:

```
CREATE INDEX idx
        ON tbl (A, B, C, ...)
     WHERE A IS NOT NULL
        OR B IS NOT NULL
        OR C IS NOT NULL
           ...;
```

Consider the EMP_DOB index. It has only one column: the DATE_OF_BIRTH. A row that does not have a DATE_OF_BIRTH value is not added to this index.

```
INSERT INTO employees ( subsidiary_id, employee_id
                      , first_name   , last_name
                      , phone_number)
              VALUES ( ?, ?, ?, ?, ? );
```

The **insert** statement does not set the DATE_OF_BIRTH so it defaults to NULL — hence, the record is not added to the EMP_DOB index. As a consequence, the index cannot support a query for records where DATE_OF_BIRTH IS NULL:

```
SELECT first_name, last_name
  FROM employees
 WHERE date_of_birth IS NULL;
```

54

```
---------------------------------------------------
| Id | Operation          | Name      | Rows | Cost |
---------------------------------------------------
|  0 | SELECT STATEMENT  |           |    1 |  477 |
|* 1 | TABLE ACCESS FULL| EMPLOYEES |    1 |  477 |
---------------------------------------------------

Predicate Information (identified by operation id):
---------------------------------------------------
   1 - filter("DATE_OF_BIRTH" IS NULL)
```

Nevertheless, the record is inserted into a concatenated index if at least one index column is not NULL:

```
CREATE INDEX demo_null
          ON employees (subsidiary_id, date_of_birth);
```

The above created row is added to the index because the SUBSIDIARY_ID is not NULL. This index can thus support a query for all employees of a specific subsidiary that have no DATE_OF_BIRTH value:

```
SELECT first_name, last_name
  FROM employees
 WHERE subsidiary_id = ?
   AND date_of_birth IS NULL;
```

```
-----------------------------------------------------------------
| Id | Operation                   | Name      | Rows | Cost |
-----------------------------------------------------------------
|  0 | SELECT STATEMENT            |           |    1 |    2 |
|  1 |  TABLE ACCESS BY INDEX ROWID| EMPLOYEES |    1 |    2 |
|* 2 |   INDEX RANGE SCAN          | DEMO_NULL |    1 |    1 |
-----------------------------------------------------------------

Predicate Information (identified by operation id):
-----------------------------------------------------------------
   2 - access("SUBSIDIARY_ID"=TO_NUMBER(?)
           AND "DATE_OF_BIRTH" IS NULL)
```

Please note that the index covers the entire **where** clause; all filters are used as access predicates during the INDEX RANGE SCAN.

We can extend this concept for the original query to find all records where DATE_OF_BIRTH IS NULL. For that, the DATE_OF_BIRTH column has to be the leftmost column in the index so that it can be used as access predicate. Although we do not need a second index column for the query itself, we add another column that can never be NULL to make sure the index has all rows.

CHAPTER 2: THE WHERE CLAUSE

We can use any column that has a NOT NULL constraint, like SUBSIDIARY_ID, for that purpose.

Alternatively, we can use a constant expression that can never be NULL. That makes sure the index has all rows—even if DATE_OF_BIRTH is NULL.

```
DROP    INDEX emp_dob;
CREATE INDEX emp_dob ON employees (date_of_birth, '1');
```

Technically, this index is a function-based index. This example also disproves the myth that the Oracle database cannot index NULL.

TIP

Add a column that cannot be NULL to index NULL like any value.

NOT NULL CONSTRAINTS

To index an IS NULL condition in the Oracle database, the index must have a column that can never be NULL.

That said, it is not enough that there are no NULL entries. The database has to be sure there can never be a NULL entry, otherwise the database must assume that the table has rows that are not in the index.

The following index supports the query only if the column LAST_NAME has a NOT NULL constraint:

```
DROP INDEX emp_dob;
CREATE INDEX emp_dob_name
          ON employees (date_of_birth, last_name);

SELECT *
  FROM employees
 WHERE date_of_birth IS NULL;
```

56

NOT NULL CONSTRAINTS

```
--------------------------------------------------------------
|Id |Operation                    | Name          | Rows | Cost |
--------------------------------------------------------------
|  0 |SELECT STATEMENT            |               |   1 |    3 |
|  1 | TABLE ACCESS BY INDEX ROWID| EMPLOYEES     |   1 |    3 |
|*2 |  INDEX RANGE SCAN          | EMP_DOB_NAME  |   1 |    2 |
--------------------------------------------------------------

Predicate Information (identified by operation id):
--------------------------------------------------
   2 - access("DATE_OF_BIRTH" IS NULL)
```

Removing the NOT NULL constraint renders the index unusable for this query:

```
ALTER TABLE employees MODIFY last_name NULL;

SELECT *
  FROM employees
 WHERE date_of_birth IS NULL;
```

```
------------------------------------------------------
| Id | Operation         | Name      | Rows | Cost |
------------------------------------------------------
|  0 | SELECT STATEMENT  |           |   1 |  477 |
|* 1 |  TABLE ACCESS FULL| EMPLOYEES |   1 |  477 |
------------------------------------------------------
```

> **TIP**
>
> A missing NOT NULL constraint can prevent index usage in an Oracle database—especially for count(*) queries.

Besides NOT NULL constraints, the database also knows that constant expressions like in the previous section cannot become NULL.

An index on a user-defined function, however, does not impose a NOT NULL constraint on the index expression:

```
CREATE OR REPLACE FUNCTION blackbox(id IN NUMBER) RETURN NUMBER
DETERMINISTIC
IS BEGIN
    RETURN id;
END;

DROP INDEX emp_dob_name;
CREATE INDEX emp_dob_bb
    ON employees (date_of_birth, blackbox(employee_id));
```

CHAPTER 2: THE WHERE CLAUSE

```
SELECT *
  FROM employees
 WHERE date_of_birth IS NULL;

---------------------------------------------------
| Id | Operation        | Name        | Rows | Cost |
---------------------------------------------------
|  0 | SELECT STATEMENT |             |    1 |  477 |
|* 1 | TABLE ACCESS FULL| EMPLOYEES   |    1 |  477 |
---------------------------------------------------
```

The function name BLACKBOX emphasizes the fact that the optimizer has no idea what the function does. We can see that the function passes the input value straight through, but for the database it is just a function that returns a number. The NOT NULL property of the parameter is lost. Although the index must have all rows, the database does not know that so it cannot use the index for the query.

If *you know* that the function never returns NULL, as in this example, you can change the query to reflect that:

```
SELECT *
  FROM employees
 WHERE date_of_birth IS NULL
   AND blackbox(employee_id) IS NOT NULL;

------------------------------------------------------------
|Id |Operation                     | Name       | Rows | Cost |
------------------------------------------------------------
| 0 |SELECT STATEMENT              |            |    1 |    3 |
| 1 | TABLE ACCESS BY INDEX ROWID| EMPLOYEES  |    1 |    3 |
|*2 |  INDEX RANGE SCAN            | EMP_DOB_BB |    1 |    2 |
------------------------------------------------------------
```

The extra condition in the **where** clause is always true and therefore does not change the result. Nevertheless the Oracle database recognizes that you only query rows that must be in the index per definition.

There is, unfortunately, no way to tag a function that never returns NULL but you can move the function call to a virtual column (since 11*g*) and put a NOT NULL constraint on this column.

```
ALTER TABLE employees ADD bb_expression
      GENERATED ALWAYS AS (blackbox(employee_id)) NOT NULL;

DROP   INDEX emp_dob_bb;
CREATE INDEX emp_dob_bb
    ON employees (date_of_birth, bb_expression);
```

NOT NULL CONSTRAINTS

```
SELECT *
  FROM employees
 WHERE date_of_birth IS NULL;


---------------------------------------------------------------
|Id |Operation                   | Name         | Rows | Cost |
---------------------------------------------------------------
| 0 |SELECT STATEMENT            |              |   1  |   3  |
| 1 | TABLE ACCESS BY INDEX ROWID| EMPLOYEES    |   1  |   3  |
|*2 |  INDEX RANGE SCAN          | EMP_DOB_BB   |   1  |   2  |
---------------------------------------------------------------
```

The Oracle database knows that some internal functions only return NULL
if NULL is provided as input.

```
DROP INDEX emp_dob_bb;

CREATE INDEX emp_dob_upname
    ON employees (date_of_birth, upper(last_name));

SELECT *
  FROM employees
 WHERE date_of_birth IS NULL;


---------------------------------------------------------------
|Id |Operation                   | Name           | Cost |
---------------------------------------------------------------
| 0 |SELECT STATEMENT            |                |   3  |
| 1 | TABLE ACCESS BY INDEX ROWID| EMPLOYEES      |   3  |
|*2 |  INDEX RANGE SCAN          | EMP_DOB_UPNAME |   2  |
---------------------------------------------------------------
```

The UPPER function preserves the NOT NULL property of the LAST_NAME
column. Removing the constraint, however, renders the index unusable:

```
ALTER TABLE employees MODIFY last_name NULL;

SELECT *
  FROM employees
 WHERE date_of_birth IS NULL;


--------------------------------------------------------
| Id | Operation        | Name      | Rows | Cost |
--------------------------------------------------------
| 0  | SELECT STATEMENT |           |   1  |  477 |
|* 1 |  TABLE ACCESS FULL| EMPLOYEES |   1  |  477 |
--------------------------------------------------------
```

EMULATING PARTIAL INDEXES

The strange way the Oracle database handles NULL in indexes can be used to emulate partial indexes. For that, we just have to use NULL for rows that should not be indexed.

To demonstrate, we emulate the following partial index:

```
CREATE INDEX messages_todo
        ON messages (receiver)
     WHERE processed = 'N'
```

First, we need a function that returns the RECEIVER value only if the PROCESSED value is 'N'.

```
CREATE OR REPLACE
FUNCTION pi_processed(processed CHAR, receiver NUMBER)
RETURN NUMBER
DETERMINISTIC
AS BEGIN
   IF processed IN ('N') THEN
       RETURN receiver;
   ELSE
       RETURN NULL;
   END IF;
END;
/
```

The function must be deterministic so it can be used in an index definition.

Now we can create an index that contains only the rows having PROCESSED='N'.

```
CREATE INDEX messages_todo
        ON messages (pi_processed(processed, receiver));
```

EMULATING PARTIAL INDEXES

To use the index, you must use the indexed expression in the query:

```
SELECT message
  FROM messages
 WHERE pi_processed(processed, receiver) = ?

-----------------------------------------------------------
|Id | Operation                     | Name         | Cost |
-----------------------------------------------------------
| 0 | SELECT STATEMENT              |              | 5330 |
| 1 |  TABLE ACCESS BY INDEX ROWID| MESSAGES       | 5330 |
|*2 |   INDEX RANGE SCAN            | MESSAGES_TODO | 5303 |
-----------------------------------------------------------

Predicate Information (identified by operation id):
---------------------------------------------------
   2 - access("PI_PROCESSED"("PROCESSED","RECEIVER")=:X)
```

PARTIAL INDEXES, PART II

As of release 11g, there is a second—equally scary—approach to emulating partial indexes in the Oracle database by using an intentionally broken index partition and the SKIP_UNUSABLE_INDEX parameter.

CHAPTER 2: THE WHERE CLAUSE

Obfuscated Conditions

The following sections demonstrate some popular methods for obfuscating conditions. Obfuscated conditions are **where** clauses that are phrased in a way that prevents proper index usage. This section is a collection of anti-patterns every developer should know about and avoid.

Date Types

Most obfuscations involve DATE types. The Oracle database is particularly vulnerable in this respect because it has only one DATE type that always includes a time component as well.

It has become common practice to use the TRUNC function to remove the time component. In truth, it does not remove the time but instead sets it to midnight because the Oracle database has no pure DATE type. To disregard the time component for a search you can use the TRUNC function on both sides of the comparison—e.g., to search for yesterday's sales:

```
SELECT ...
  FROM sales
 WHERE TRUNC(sale_date) = TRUNC(sysdate - INTERVAL '1' DAY)
```

It is a perfectly valid and correct statement but it cannot properly make use of an index on SALE_DATE. It is as explained in "Case-Insensitive Search Using UPPER or LOWER" on page 24; TRUNC(sale_date) is something entirely different from SALE_DATE—functions are black boxes to the database.

There is a rather simple solution for this problem: a function-based index.

```
CREATE INDEX index_name
          ON sales (TRUNC(sale_date))
```

But then you must always use TRUNC(sale_date) in the **where** clause. If you use it inconsistently—sometimes with, sometimes without TRUNC—then you need two indexes!

62

DATE TYPES

The problem also occurs with databases that have a pure date type if you search for a longer period as shown in the following MySQL query:

```
SELECT ...
  FROM sales
 WHERE DATE_FORMAT(sale_date, "%Y-%M")
     = DATE_FORMAT(now()    , "%Y-%M")
```

The query uses a date format that only contains year and month: again, this is an absolutely correct query that has the same problem as before. However the solution from above does not apply here because MySQL has no function-based indexes.

The alternative is to use an explicit range condition. This is a generic solution that works for all databases:

```
SELECT ...
  FROM sales
 WHERE sale_date BETWEEN quarter_begin(?)
                     AND quarter_end(?)
```

If you have done your homework, you probably recognize the pattern from the exercise about all employees who are 42 years old.

A straight index on SALE_DATE is enough to optimize this query. The functions QUARTER_BEGIN and QUARTER_END compute the boundary dates. The calculation can become a little complex because the **between** operator always includes the boundary values. The QUARTER_END function must therefore return a time stamp just before the first day of the next quarter if the SALE_DATE has a time component. This logic can be hidden in the function.

The examples on the following pages show implementations of the functions QUARTER_BEGIN and QUARTER_END for various databases.

63

MySQL

```
CREATE FUNCTION quarter_begin(dt DATETIME)
RETURNS DATETIME DETERMINISTIC
RETURN CONVERT
        (
          CONCAT
          ( CONVERT(YEAR(dt),CHAR(4))
          , '-'
          , CONVERT(QUARTER(dt)*3-2,CHAR(2))
          , '-01'
          )
        , datetime
        );

CREATE FUNCTION quarter_end(dt DATETIME)
RETURNS DATETIME DETERMINISTIC
RETURN DATE_ADD
        ( DATE_ADD ( quarter_begin(dt), INTERVAL 3 MONTH )
        , INTERVAL -1 MICROSECOND);
```

Oracle Database

```
CREATE FUNCTION quarter_begin(dt IN DATE)
RETURN DATE
AS
BEGIN
    RETURN TRUNC(dt, 'Q');
END;
/

CREATE FUNCTION quarter_end(dt IN DATE)
RETURN DATE
AS
BEGIN
    -- the Oracle DATE type has seconds resolution
    -- subtract one second from the first
    -- day of the following quarter
    RETURN TRUNC(ADD_MONTHS(dt, +3), 'Q')
        - (1/(24*60*60));
END;
/
```

DATE TYPES

POSTGRESQL

```
CREATE FUNCTION quarter_begin(dt timestamp with time zone)
RETURNS timestamp with time zone AS $$
BEGIN
    RETURN date_trunc('quarter', dt);
END;
$$ LANGUAGE plpgsql;

CREATE FUNCTION quarter_end(dt timestamp with time zone)
RETURNS timestamp with time zone AS $$
BEGIN
   RETURN   date_trunc('quarter', dt)
            + interval '3 month'
            - interval '1 microsecond';
END;
$$ LANGUAGE plpgsql;
```

SQL SERVER

```
CREATE FUNCTION quarter_begin (@dt DATETIME )
RETURNS DATETIME
BEGIN
  RETURN DATEADD (qq, DATEDIFF (qq, 0, @dt), 0)
END
GO

CREATE FUNCTION quarter_end (@dt DATETIME )
RETURNS DATETIME
BEGIN
  RETURN DATEADD
          ( ms
          , -3
          , DATEADD(mm, 3, dbo.quarter_begin(@dt))
          );
END
GO
```

You can use similar auxiliary functions for other periods—most of them will be less complex than the examples above, especially when using greater than or equal to (>=) and less than (<) conditions instead of the **between** operator. Of course you could calculate the boundary dates in your application if you wish.

65

CHAPTER 2: THE WHERE CLAUSE

> **TIP**
>
> Write queries for continuous periods as explicit range condition. Do this even for a single day—e.g., for the Oracle database:
>
> ```
>     sale_date >= TRUNC(sysdate)
> AND sale_date <  TRUNC(sysdate + INTERVAL '1' DAY)
> ```

Another common obfuscation is to compare dates as strings as shown in the following PostgreSQL example:

```
SELECT ...
  FROM sales
 WHERE TO_CHAR(sale_date, 'YYYY-MM-DD') = '1970-01-01'
```

The problem is, again, converting SALE_DATE. Such conditions are often created in the belief that you cannot pass different types than numbers and strings to the database. Bind parameters, however, support all data types. That means you can for example use a java.util.Date object as bind parameter. This is yet another benefit of bind parameters.

If you cannot do that, you just have to convert the search term instead of the table column:

```
SELECT ...
  FROM sales
 WHERE sale_date = TO_DATE('1970-01-01', 'YYYY-MM-DD')
```

This query can use a straight index on SALE_DATE. Moreover it converts the input string only once. The previous statement must convert all dates stored in the table before it can compare them against the search term.

Whatever change you make—using a bind parameter or converting the other side of the comparison—you can easily introduce a bug if SALE_DATE has a time component. You must use an explicit range condition in that case:

```
SELECT ...
  FROM sales
 WHERE sale_date >= TO_DATE('1970-01-01', 'YYYY-MM-DD')
   AND sale_date <  TO_DATE('1970-01-01', 'YYYY-MM-DD')
                    + INTERVAL '1' DAY
```

Always consider using an explicit range condition when comparing dates.

66

LIKE ON DATE TYPES

The following obfuscation is particularly tricky:

```
sale_date LIKE SYSDATE
```

It does not look like an obfuscation at first glance because it does not use any functions.

The LIKE operator, however, enforces a string comparison. Depending on the database, that might yield an error or cause an implicit type conversion on both sides. The "Predicate Information" section of the execution plan shows what the Oracle database does:

```
filter( INTERNAL_FUNCTION(SALE_DATE)
   LIKE TO_CHAR(SYSDATE@!))
```

The function INTERNAL_FUNCTION converts the type of the SALE_DATE column. As a side effect it also prevents using a straight index on DATE_COLUMN *just as any other function would.*

Numeric Strings

Numeric strings are numbers that are stored in text columns. Although it is a very bad practice, it does not automatically render an index useless if you consistently treat it as string:

```
SELECT ...
  FROM ...
 WHERE numeric_string = '42'
```

Of course this statement can use an index on NUMERIC_STRING. If you compare it using a number, however, the database can no longer use this condition as an access predicate.

```
SELECT ...
  FROM ...
 WHERE numeric_string = 42
```

Note the missing quotes. Although some database yield an error (e.g. PostgreSQL) many databases just add an implicit type conversion.

```
SELECT ...
  FROM ...
 WHERE TO_NUMBER(numeric_string) = 42
```

It is the same problem as before. An index on NUMERIC_STRING cannot be used due to the function call. The solution is also the same as before: do not convert the table column, instead convert the search term.

```
SELECT ...
  FROM ...
 WHERE numeric_string = TO_CHAR(42)
```

You might wonder why the database does not do it this way automatically? It is because converting a string to a number always gives an unambiguous result. This is not true the other way around. A number, formatted as text, can contain spaces, punctuation, and leading zeros. A single value can be written in many ways:

```
42
042
0042
00042
...
```

The database cannot know the number format used in the NUMERIC_STRING column so it does it the other way around: the database converts the strings to numbers—this is an unambiguous transformation.

The TO_CHAR function returns only one string representation of the number. It will therefore only match the first of above listed strings. If we use TO_NUMBER, it matches all of them. That means there is not only a performance difference between the two variants but also a semantic difference!

Using numeric strings is generally troublesome: most importantly it causes performance problems due to the implicit conversion and also introduces a risk of running into conversion errors due to invalid numbers. Even the most trivial query that does not use any functions in the **where** clause can cause an abort with a conversion error if there is just one invalid number stored in the table.

> **TIP**
>
> Use numeric types to store numbers.

Note that the problem does not exist the other way around:

```
SELECT ...
  FROM ...
 WHERE numeric_number = '42'
```

The database will consistently transform the string into a number. It does not apply a function on the potentially indexed column: a regular index will therefore work. Nevertheless it is possible to do a manual conversion the wrong way:

```
SELECT ...
  FROM ...
 WHERE TO_CHAR(numeric_number) = '42'
```

CHAPTER 2: THE WHERE CLAUSE

COMBINING COLUMNS

This section is about a popular obfuscation that affects concatenated indexes.

The first example is again about date and time types but the other way around. The following MySQL query combines a data and a time column to apply a range filter on both of them.

```
SELECT ...
  FROM ...
 WHERE ADDTIME(date_column, time_column)
     > DATE_ADD(now(), INTERVAL -1 DAY)
```

It selects all records from the last 24 hours. The query cannot use a concatenated index on (DATE_COLUMN, TIME_COLUMN) properly because the search is not done on the indexed columns but on derived data.

You can avoid this problem by using a data type that has both a date and time component (e.g., MySQL DATETIME). You can then use this column without a function call:

```
SELECT ...
  FROM ...
 WHERE datetime_column
     > DATE_ADD(now(), INTERVAL -1 DAY)
```

Unfortunately it is often not possible to change the table when facing this problem.

The next option is a function-based index if the database supports it—although this has all the drawbacks discussed before. When using MySQL, function-based indexes are not an option anyway.

It is still possible to write the query so that the database can use a concatenated index on DATE_COLUMN, TIME_COLUMN with an access predicate—at least partially. For that, we add an extra condition on the DATE_COLUMN.

```
 WHERE ADDTIME(date_column, time_column)
     > DATE_ADD(now(), INTERVAL -1 DAY)
   AND date_column
    >= DATE(DATE_ADD(now(), INTERVAL -1 DAY))
```

70

COMBINING COLUMNS

The new condition is absolutely redundant but it is a straight filter on DATE_COLUMN that can be used as access predicate. Even though this technique is not perfect, it is usually a good enough approximation.

> **TIP**
>
> Use a redundant condition on the most significant column when a range condition combines multiple columns.
>
> For PostgreSQL, it's preferable to use the row values syntax described on page 151.

You can also use this technique when storing date and time in text columns, but you have to use date and time formats that yields a chronological order when sorted lexically—e.g., as suggested by ISO 8601 (YYYY-MM-DD HH:MM:SS). The following example uses the Oracle database's TO_CHAR function for that purpose:

```
SELECT ...
  FROM ...
 WHERE date_string || time_string
     > TO_CHAR(sysdate - 1, 'YYYY-MM-DD HH24:MI:SS')
   AND date_string
    >= TO_CHAR(sysdate - 1, 'YYYY-MM-DD')
```

We will face the problem of applying a range condition over multiple columns again in the section entitled "Paging Through Results". We'll also use the same approximation method to mitigate it.

Sometimes we have the reverse case and might want to obfuscate a condition intentionally so it cannot be used anymore as access predicate. We already looked at that problem when discussing the effects of bind parameters on LIKE conditions. Consider the following example:

```
SELECT last_name, first_name, employee_id
  FROM employees
 WHERE subsidiary_id = ?
   AND last_name LIKE ?
```

Assuming there is an index on SUBSIDIARY_ID and another one on LAST_NAME, which one is better for this query?

71

CHAPTER 2: THE WHERE CLAUSE

Without knowing the wildcard's position in the search term, it is impossible to give a qualified answer. The optimizer has no other choice than to "guess". If *you know* that there is always a leading wildcard, you can obfuscate the LIKE condition intentionally so that the optimizer can no longer consider the index on LAST_NAME.

```
SELECT last_name, first_name, employee_id
  FROM employees
 WHERE subsidiary_id = ?
   AND last_name || '' LIKE ?
```

It is enough to append an empty string to the LAST_NAME column. This is, however, an option of last resort. Only do it when absolutely necessary.

SMART LOGIC

One of the key features of SQL databases is their support for ad-hoc queries: new queries can be executed at any time. This is only possible because the query optimizer (query planner) works at runtime; it analyzes each statement when received and generates a reasonable execution plan immediately. The overhead introduced by runtime optimization can be minimized with bind parameters.

The gist of that recap is that databases are optimized for dynamic SQL—so use it if you need it.

Nevertheless there is a widely used practice that avoids dynamic SQL in favor of static SQL—often because of the "dynamic SQL is slow" myth. This practice does more harm than good if the database uses a shared execution plan cache like DB2, the Oracle database, or SQL Server.

For the sake of demonstration, imagine an application that queries the EMPLOYEES table. The application allows searching for subsidiary id, employee id and last name (case-insensitive) in any combination. It is still possible to write a single query that covers all cases by using "smart" logic.

72

SMART LOGIC

```
SELECT first_name, last_name, subsidiary_id, employee_id
  FROM employees
 WHERE ( subsidiary_id   = :sub_id OR :sub_id IS NULL )
   AND ( employee_id      = :emp_id OR :emp_id IS NULL )
   AND ( UPPER(last_name) = :name   OR :name   IS NULL )
```

The query uses named bind variables for better readability. All possible filter expressions are statically coded in the statement. Whenever a filter isn't needed, you just use NULL instead of a search term: it disables the condition via the OR logic.

It is a perfectly reasonable SQL statement. The use of NULL is even in line with its definition according to the three-valued logic of SQL. Nevertheless it is one of the *worst performance anti-patterns* of all.

The database cannot optimize the execution plan for a particular filter because any of them could be canceled out at runtime. The database needs to prepare for the worst case — if all filters are disabled:

```
---------------------------------------------------
| Id | Operation       | Name      | Rows | Cost |
---------------------------------------------------
|  0 | SELECT STATEMENT |          |    2 |  478 |
|* 1 | TABLE ACCESS FULL| EMPLOYEES |    2 |  478 |
---------------------------------------------------

Predicate Information (identified by operation id):
---------------------------------------------------
1 - filter((:NAME    IS NULL OR UPPER("LAST_NAME")=:NAME)
       AND (:EMP_ID IS NULL OR "EMPLOYEE_ID"=:EMP_ID)
       AND (:SUB_ID IS NULL OR "SUBSIDIARY_ID"=:SUB_ID))
```

As a consequence, the database uses a full table scan *even if there is an index for each column.*

It is not that the database cannot resolve the "smart" logic. It creates the generic execution plan due to the use of bind parameters so it can be cached and re-used with other values later on. If we do not use bind parameters but write the actual values in the SQL statement, the optimizer selects the proper index for the active filter:

```
SELECT first_name, last_name, subsidiary_id, employee_id
  FROM employees
 WHERE( subsidiary_id   = NULL    OR NULL IS NULL )
   AND( employee_id      = NULL    OR NULL IS NULL )
   AND( UPPER(last_name) = 'WINAND' OR 'WINAND' IS NULL )
```

73

CHAPTER 2: THE WHERE CLAUSE

```
---------------------------------------------------------------
|Id | Operation                  | Name        | Rows | Cost |
---------------------------------------------------------------
| 0 | SELECT STATEMENT           |             |    1 |    2 |
| 1 |  TABLE ACCESS BY INDEX ROWID| EMPLOYEES   |    1 |    2 |
|*2 |   INDEX RANGE SCAN          | EMP_UP_NAME |    1 |    1 |
---------------------------------------------------------------

Predicate Information (identified by operation id):
---------------------------------------------------
   2 - access(UPPER("LAST_NAME")='WINAND')
```

This, however, is no solution. It just proves that the database can resolve these conditions.

> **WARNING**
>
> Using literal values makes your application vulnerable to SQL injection attacks and can cause performance problems due to increased optimization overhead.

The obvious solution for dynamic queries is dynamic SQL. According to the KISS principle[3], just tell the database what you need right now—and nothing else.

```
SELECT first_name, last_name, subsidiary_id, employee_id
  FROM employees
 WHERE UPPER(last_name) = :name
```

Note that the query uses a bind parameter.

> **TIP**
>
> Use dynamic SQL if you need dynamic where clauses.
>
> Still use bind parameters when generating dynamic SQL—otherwise the "dynamic SQL is slow" myth comes true.

The problem described in this section is widespread. All databases that use a shared execution plan cache have a feature to cope with it—often introducing new problems and bugs.

---

[3] http://en.wikipedia.org/wiki/KISS_principle

74

MySQL

MySQL does not suffer from this particular problem because it has no execution plan cache at all. A feature request from 2009 discusses the impact of execution plan caching. It seems that MySQL's optimizer is simple enough so that execution plan caching does not pay off.

ORACLE DATABASE

The Oracle database uses a shared execution plan cache ("SQL area") and is fully exposed to the problem described in this section.

Oracle introduced the so-called *bind peeking* with release 9*i*. Bind peeking enables the optimizer to use the actual bind values of the first execution when preparing an execution plan. The problem with this approach is its nondeterministic behavior: the values from the first execution affect all executions. The execution plan can change whenever the database is restarted or, less predictably, the cached plan expires and the optimizer recreates it using different values the next time the statement is executed.

Release 11*g* introduced *adaptive cursor sharing* to further improve the situation. This feature allows the database to cache multiple execution plans for the same SQL statement. Further, the optimizer peeks the bind parameters and stores their estimated selectivity along with the execution plan. When the cache is subsequently accessed, the selectivity of the current bind values must fall within the selectivity ranges of a cached execution plan to be reused. Otherwise the optimizer creates a new execution plan and compares it against the already cached execution plans for this query. If there is already such an execution plan, the database replaces it with a new execution plan that also covers the selectivity estimates of the current bind values. If not, it caches a new execution plan variant for this query — along with the selectivity estimates, of course.

PostgreSQL

The PostgreSQL query plan cache works for open statements only — that is as long as you keep the PreparedStatement open. The above described problem occurs only when re-using a statement handle. Note that PostgresSQL's JDBC driver enables the cache after the fifth execution only.

CHAPTER 2: THE WHERE CLAUSE

SQL SERVER

SQL Server uses so-called *parameter sniffing*. Parameter sniffing enables the optimizer to use the actual bind values of the first execution during parsing. The problem with this approach is its nondeterministic behavior: the values from the first execution affect all executions. The execution plan can change whenever the database is restarted or, less predictably, the cached plan expires and the optimizer recreates it using different values the next time the statement is executed.

SQL Server 2005 added new query hints to gain more control over parameter sniffing and recompiling. The query hint RECOMPILE bypasses the plan cache for a selected statement. OPTIMIZE FOR allows the specification of actual parameter values that are used for optimization only. Finally, you can provide an entire execution plan with the USE PLAN hint.

The original implementation of the OPTION(RECOMPILE) hint had a bug so it did not consider all bind variables. The new implementation introduced with SQL Server 2008 had another bug, making the situation very confusing. Erland Sommarskog[4] has collected the all relevant information covering all SQL Server releases.

Although heuristic methods can improve the "smart logic" problem to a certain extent, they were actually built to deal with the problems of bind parameter in connection with column histograms and LIKE expressions.

The most reliable method for arriving at the best execution plan is to avoid unnecessary filters in the SQL statement.

---

[4] http://www.sommarskog.se/dyn-search-2008.html

MATH

There is one more class of obfuscations that is smart and prevents proper index usage. Instead of using logic expressions it is using a calculation.

Consider the following statement. Can it use an index on NUMERIC_NUMBER?

```
SELECT numeric_number
  FROM table_name
 WHERE numeric_number - 1000 > ?
```

Similarly, can the following statement use an index on A and B—you choose the order?

```
SELECT a, b
  FROM table_name
 WHERE 3*a + 5 = b
```

Let's put these questions into a different perspective; if you were developing an SQL database, would you add an equation solver? Most database vendors just say "No!" and thus, neither of the two examples uses the index.

You can even use math to obfuscate a condition intentionally—as we did it previously for the full text LIKE search. It is enough to add zero, for example:

```
SELECT numeric_number
  FROM table_name
 WHERE numeric_number + 0 = ?
```

Nevertheless we can index these expressions with a function-based index if we use calculations in a smart way and transform the **where** clause like an equation:

```
SELECT a, b
  FROM table_name
 WHERE 3*a - b = -5
```

We just moved the table references to the one side and the constants to the other. We can then create a function-based index for the left hand side of the equation:

```
CREATE INDEX math ON table_name (3*a - b)
```

CHAPTER 3

PERFORMANCE AND SCALABILITY

This chapter is about performance and scalability of databases.

In this context, I am using the following definition for scalability:

> *Scalability is the ability of a system, network, or process,*
> *to handle a growing amount of work in a capable manner*
> *or*
> *its ability to be enlarged to accommodate that growth.*
>
> —Wikipedia[1]

You see that there are actually two definitions. The first one is about the effects of a growing load on a system and the second is about growing a system to handle more load.

The second definition enjoys much more popularity than the first one. Whenever somebody talks about scalability, it is almost always about using more hardware. *Scale-up* and *scale-out* are the respective keywords which were recently complemented by new buzzwords like *web-scale*.

Broadly speaking, scalability is about the performance impact of environmental changes. Hardware is just one environmental parameter that can change. This chapter covers other parameters like data volume and system load as well.

---

[1] http://en.wikipedia.org/wiki/Scalability

PERFORMANCE IMPACTS OF DATA VOLUME

The amount of data stored in a database has a great impact on its performance. It is usually accepted that a query becomes slower with additional data in the database. But how great is the performance impact if the data volume doubles? And how can we improve this ratio? These are the key questions when discussing database scalability.

As an example we analyze the response time of the following query when using two different indexes. The index definitions will remain unknown for the time being—they will be revealed during the course of the discussion.

```
SELECT count(*)
  FROM scale_data
 WHERE section = ?
   AND id2 = ?
```

The column SECTION has a special purpose in this query: it controls the data volume. The bigger the SECTION number becomes, the more rows the query selects. Figure 3.1 shows the response time for a small SECTION.

Figure 3.1. Performance Comparison

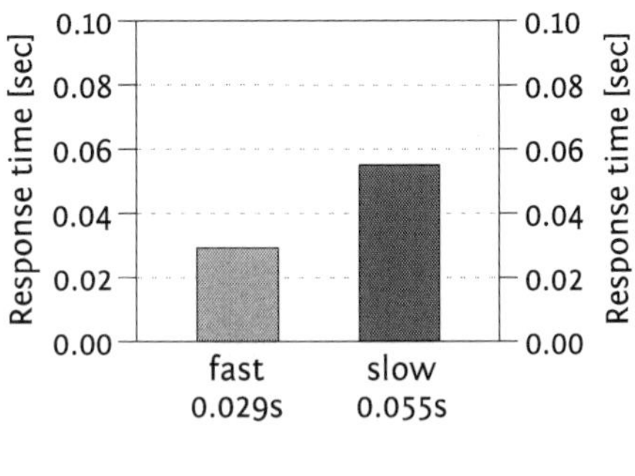

There is a considerable performance difference between the two indexing variants. Both response times are still well below a tenth of a second so even the slower query is probably fast enough in most cases. However the performance chart shows only one test point. Discussing scalability means to look at the performance impact when changing environmental parameters—such as the data volume.

PERFORMANCE IMPACTS OF DATA VOLUME

> **IMPORTANT**
>
> Scalability shows the dependency of performance on factors like the data volume.
>
> A performance value is just a single data point on a scalability chart.

Figure 3.2 shows the response time over the SECTION number—that means for a growing data volume.

Figure 3.2. Scalability by Data Volume

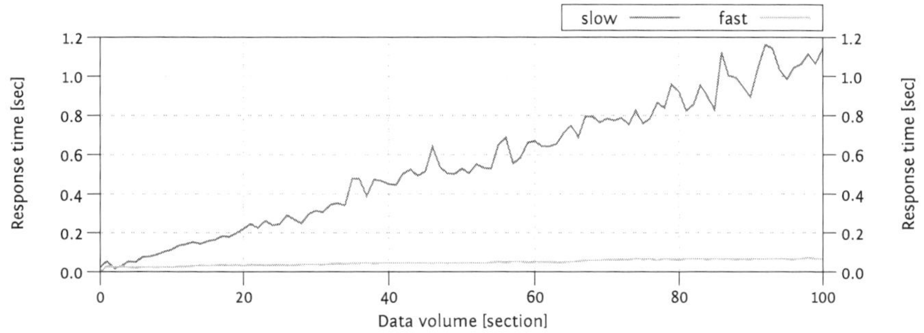

The chart shows a growing response time for both indexes. On the right hand side of the chart, when the data volume is a hundred times as high, the faster query needs more than twice as long as it originally did while the response time of the slower query increased by a factor of 20 to more than one second.

The response time of an SQL query depends on many factors. The data volume is one of them. If a query is fast enough under certain testing conditions, it does not mean it will be fast enough in production. That is especially the case in development environments that have only a fraction of the data of the production system.

It is, however, no surprise that the queries get slower when the data volume grows. But the striking gap between the two indexes is somewhat unexpected. What is the reason for the different growth rates?

CHAPTER 3: PERFORMANCE AND SCALABILITY

It should be easy to find the reason by comparing both execution plans.

```
---------------------------------------------------------
| Id | Operation        | Name        | Rows  | Cost |
---------------------------------------------------------
|  0 | SELECT STATEMENT |             |     1 |  972 |
|  1 |  SORT AGGREGATE  |             |     1 |      |
|* 2 |   INDEX RANGE SCAN| SCALE_SLOW | 3000  |  972 |
---------------------------------------------------------


---------------------------------------------------------
| Id   Operation        | Name        | Rows  | Cost |
---------------------------------------------------------
|  0 | SELECT STATEMENT |             |     1 |   13 |
|  1 |  SORT AGGREGATE  |             |     1 |      |
|* 2 |   INDEX RANGE SCAN| SCALE_FAST | 3000  |   13 |
---------------------------------------------------------
```

The execution plans are almost identical—they just use a different index. Even though the cost values reflect the speed difference, the reason is not visible in the execution plan.

It seems like we are facing a "slow index experience"; the query is slow although it uses an index. Nevertheless we do not believe in the myth of the "broken index" anymore. Instead, we remember the two ingredients that make an index lookup slow: (1) the table access, and (2) scanning a wide index range.

Neither execution plan shows a TABLE ACCESS BY INDEX ROWID operation so one execution plan must scan a wider index range than the other. So where does an execution plan show the scanned index range? In the predicate information of course!

TIP

Pay attention to the predicate information.

The predicate information is by no means an unnecessary detail you can omit as was done above. An execution plan without predicate information is incomplete. That means you cannot see the reason for the performance difference in the plans shown above. If we look at the complete execution plans, we can see the difference.

82

PERFORMANCE IMPACTS OF DATA VOLUME

```
-------------------------------------------------------
| Id | Operation         | Name       | Rows | Cost |
-------------------------------------------------------
|  0 | SELECT STATEMENT  |            |    1 |  972 |
|  1 |  SORT AGGREGATE   |            |    1 |      |
|* 2 |   INDEX RANGE SCAN| SCALE_SLOW | 3000 |  972 |
-------------------------------------------------------

Predicate Information (identified by operation id):
   2 - access("SECTION"=TO_NUMBER(:A))
       filter("ID2"=TO_NUMBER(:B))


-------------------------------------------------------
| Id   Operation         | Name       | Rows | Cost |
-------------------------------------------------------
|  0 | SELECT STATEMENT  |            |    1 |   13 |
|  1 |  SORT AGGREGATE   |            |    1 |      |
|* 2 |   INDEX RANGE SCAN| SCALE_FAST | 3000 |   13 |
-------------------------------------------------------

Predicate Information (identified by operation id):
   2 - access("SECTION"=TO_NUMBER(:A) AND "ID2"=TO_NUMBER(:B))
```

> **NOTE**
>
> The execution plan was simplified for clarity. The appendix on page 170 explains the details of the "Predicate Information" section in an Oracle execution plan.

The difference is obvious now: only the condition on SECTION is an access predicate when using the SCALE_SLOW index. The database reads all rows from the section and discards those not matching the filter predicate on ID2. The response time grows with the number of rows in the section. With the SCALE_FAST index, the database uses all conditions as access predicates. The response time grows with the number of selected rows.

> **IMPORTANT**
>
> Filter predicates are like unexploded ordnance devices. They can explode at any time.

The last missing pieces in our puzzle are the index definitions. Can we reconstruct the index definitions from the execution plans?

83

CHAPTER 3: PERFORMANCE AND SCALABILITY

The definition of the SCALE_SLOW index must start with the column SECTION—otherwise it could not be used as access predicate. The condition on ID2 is not an access predicate—so it cannot follow SECTION in the index definition. That means the SCALE_SLOW index must have minimally three columns where SECTION is the first and ID2 not the second. That is exactly how it is in the index definition used for this test:

```
CREATE INDEX scale_slow ON scale_data (section, id1, id2);
```

The database cannot use ID2 as access predicate due to column ID1 in the second position.

The definition of the SCALE_FAST index must have columns SECTION and ID2 in the first two positions because both are used for access predicates. We can nonetheless not say anything about their order. The index that was used for the test starts with the SECTION column and has the extra column ID1 in the third position:

```
CREATE INDEX scale_fast ON scale_data (section, id2, id1);
```

The column ID1 was just added so this index has the same size as SCALE_SLOW—otherwise you might get the impression the size causes the difference.

84

PERFORMANCE IMPACTS OF SYSTEM LOAD

Consideration as to how to define a multi column index often stops as soon as the index is used for the query being tuned. However, the optimizer is not using an index because it is the "right" one for the query, rather because it is more efficient than a full table scan. That does not mean it is the optimal index for the query.

The previous example has shown the difficulties in recognizing incorrect column order in an execution plan. Very often the predicate information is well hidden so you have to search for it specifically to verify optimal index usage.

SQL Server Management Studio, for example, only shows the predicate information as a tool tip when moving the mouse cursor over the index operation ("hover"). The following execution plan uses the SCALE_SLOW index; it thus shows the condition on ID2 as filter predicate (just "Predicate", without Seek).

Figure 3.3. Predicate Information as a Tool Tip

Index Seek (NonClustered)	
Scan a particular range of rows from a nonclustered index.	
Physical Operation	Index Seek
Logical Operation	Index Seek
Estimated I/O Cost	0.540003
Estimated CPU Cost	0.170208
Estimated Number of Executions	1
Estimated Operator Cost	0.710211 (96%)
Estimated Subtree Cost	0.710211
Estimated Number of Rows	1545.92
Estimated Row Size	16 B
Ordered	True
Node ID	2

Predicate
[ts].[dbo].[scale_data].[id2]=[@id2]
Object
[ts].[dbo].[scale_data].[scale_slow]
Seek Predicates
Seek Keys[1]: Prefix: [ts].[dbo].[scale_data].section =
Scalar Operator([@sec])

Obtaining the predicate information from a MySQL or PostgreSQL execution plan is even more awkward. Appendix A on page 165 has the details.

85

CHAPTER 3: PERFORMANCE AND SCALABILITY

No matter how insignificant the predicate information appears in the execution plan, it has a great impact on performance—especially when the system grows. Remember that it is not only the data volume that grows but also the access rate. This is yet another parameter of the scalability function.

Figure 3.4 plots the response time as a function of the access rate—the data volume remains unchanged. It is showing the execution time of the same query as before and always uses the section with the greatest data volume. That means the last point from Figure 3.2 on page 81 corresponds with the first point in this chart.

Figure 3.4. Scalability by System Load

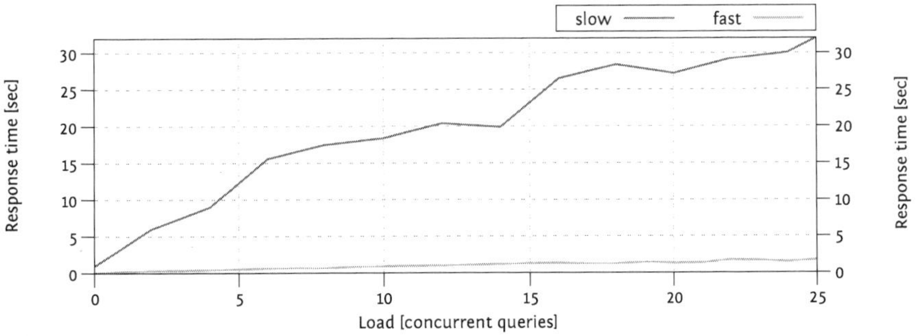

The dashed line plots the response time when using the SCALE_SLOW index. It grows by up to 32 seconds if there are 25 queries running at the same time. In comparison to the response time without background load—as it might be the case in your development environment—it takes 30 times as long. Even if you have a full copy of the production database in your development environment, the background load can still cause a query to run much slower in production.

The solid line shows the response time using the SCALE_FAST index—it does not have any filter predicates. The response time stays well below two seconds even if there are 25 queries running concurrently.

NOTE

Careful execution plan inspection yields more confidence than *superficial* benchmarks.

A full stress test is still worthwhile—but the costs are high.

86

Suspicious response times are often taken lightly during development. This is largely because we expect the "more powerful production hardware" to deliver better performance. More often than not it is the other way around because the production infrastructure is more complex and accumulates latencies that do not occur in the development environment. Even when testing on a production equivalent infrastructure, the background load can still cause different response times. In the next section we will see that it is in general not reasonable to expect faster responses from "bigger hardware".

Response Time and Throughput

Bigger hardware is not always faster—but it can usually handle more load. Bigger hardware is more like a wider highway than a faster car: you cannot drive faster—well, you are not allowed to—just because there are more lanes. That is the reason that more hardware does not automatically improve slow SQL queries.

We are not in the 1990s anymore. The computing power of single core CPUs was increasing rapidly at that time. Most response time issues disappeared on newer hardware—just because of the improved CPU. It was like new car models consistently going twice as fast as old models—every year! However, single core CPU power hit the wall during the first few years of the 21st century. There was almost no improvement on this axis anymore. To continue building ever more powerful CPUs, the vendors had to move to a multi-core strategy. Even though it allows multiple tasks to run concurrently, it does not improve performance if there is only one task. Performance has more than just one dimension.

Scaling horizontally (adding more servers) has similar limitations. Although more servers can process more requests, they do not the improve response time for one particular query. To make searching faster, you need an efficient search tree—even in non-relational systems like CouchDB and MongoDB.

Important

Proper indexing is the best way to reduce query response time—in relational SQL databases as well as in non-relational systems.

CHAPTER 3: PERFORMANCE AND SCALABILITY

Proper indexing aims to fully exploit the logarithmic scalability of the B-tree index. Unfortunately indexing is usually done in a very sloppy way. The chart in "Performance Impacts of Data Volume" makes the effect of sloppy indexing apparent.

Figure 3.5. Response Time by Data Volume

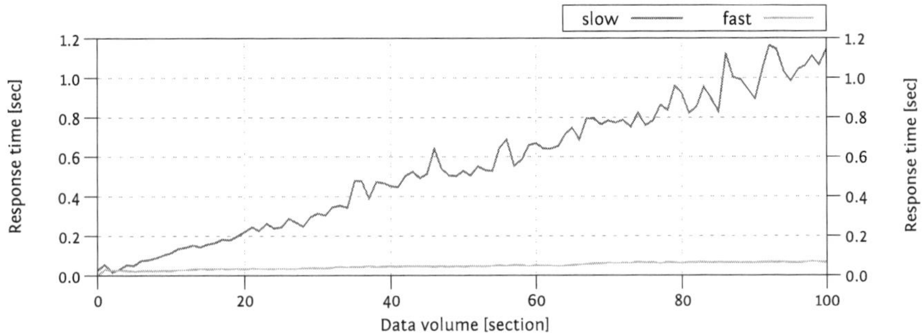

The response time difference between a sloppy and a proper index is stunning. It is hardly possible to compensate for this effect by adding more hardware. Even if you manage to cut the response time with hardware, it is still questionable if it is the best solution for this problem.

Many of the so-called NoSQL systems still claim so solve all performance problems with horizontal scalability. This scalability however is mostly limited to write operations and is accomplished with the so-called eventual consistency model. SQL databases use a strict consistency model that slows down write operations, but that does not necessarily imply bad throughput. Learn more about this in the box entitled "Eventual Consistency and the CAP Theorem".

More hardware will typically not improve response times. In fact, it might even make the system slower because the additional complexity might accumulate more latencies. Network latencies won't be a problem if the application and database run on the same computer, but this setup is rather uncommon in production environments where the database and application are usually installed in dedicated hardware. Security policies might even require a firewall between the application server and the database—often doubling the network latency. The more complex the infrastructure gets, the more latencies accumulate and the slower the responses become. This effect often leads to the counterintuitive observation that the expensive production hardware is slower than the cheap desktop PC environment that was used for development.

Eventual Consistency and the CAP Theorem

Maintaining strict consistency in a distributed system requires a synchronous coordination of all write operations between the nodes. This principle has two unpleasant side effects: (1) it adds latencies and increases response times; (2) it reduces the overall availability because multiple members must be available at the same time to complete a write operation.

A *distributed* SQL database is often confused with computer clusters that use a shared storage system or master-slave replication. In fact a *distributed* database is more like a web shop that is integrated with an ERP system—often two different products from different vendors. The consistency between both systems is still a desirable goal that is often achieved using the two-phase commit (2PC) protocol. This protocol established global transactions that deliver the well-known "all-or-nothing" behavior across multiple databases. Completing a global transaction is only possible if all contributing members are available. It thus reduces the overall availability.

The more nodes a distributed system has, the more troublesome strict consistency becomes. Maintaining strict consistency is almost impossible if the system has more than a few nodes. Dropping strict consistency, on the other hand, solves the availability problem and eliminates the increased response time. The basic idea is to reestablish the global consistency after completing the write operation on a subset of the nodes. This approach leaves just one problem unsolved: it is impossible to prevent conflicts if two nodes accept contradictory changes. Consistency is eventually reached by *handling* conflicts, not by *preventing* them. In that context, consistency means that all nodes have the same data—it is not necessarily the correct or best data.

Brewer's CAP Theorem describes the general dependencies between *C*onsistency, *A*vailability, and *P*artition tolerance.

Another very important latency is the disk seek time. Spinning hard disk drives (HDD) need a rather long time to place the mechanical parts so that the requested data can be read—typically a few milliseconds. This latency occurs four times when traversing a four level B-tree—in total: a few dozen milliseconds. Although that's half an eternity for computers, it is still far below out perception threshold...when done only once. However, it is very easy to trigger hundreds or even thousands disk seeks with a single SQL statement, in particular when combining multiple tables with a join operation. Even though caching reduces the problem dramatically and new technologies like SSD decrease the seek time by an order of magnitude, joins are still generally suspected of being slow. The next chapter will therefore explain how to use indexes for efficient table joins.

SOLID STATE DISKS (SSD) AND CACHING

Solid State Disks (SSD) are a mass storage technology that uses no moving parts. The typical seek time of SSDs is by an order of magnitude faster than the seek time of HDDs. SSDs became available for enterprise storage around 2010 but, due to their high cost and limited lifetime, are not commonly used for databases.

Databases do, however, cache frequently accessed data in the main memory. This is particularly useful for data that is needed for every index access—for example the index root nodes. The database might fully cache frequently used indexes so that an index lookup does not trigger a single disk seek.

CHAPTER 4

THE JOIN OPERATION

An SQL query walks into a bar and sees two tables.
He walks up to them and asks 'Can I join you?'

—Source: Unknown

The join operation transforms data from a normalized model into a denormalized form that suits a specific processing purpose. Joining is particularly sensitive to disk seek latencies because it combines scattered data fragments. Proper indexing is again the best solution to reduce response times. The correct index however depends on which of the three common join algorithms is used for the query.

There is, however, one thing that is common to all join algorithms: they process only two tables at a time. A SQL query with more tables requires multiple steps: first building an intermediate result set by joining two tables, then joining the result with the next table and so forth.

Even though the join order has no impact on the final result, it still affects performance. The optimizer will therefore evaluate all possible join order permutations and select the best one. That means that just optimizing a complex statement might become a performance problem. The more tables to join, the more execution plan variants to evaluate—mathematically speaking: n! (factorial growth), though this is not a problem when using bind parameters.

IMPORTANT

The more complex the statement the more important using bind parameters becomes.

Not using bind parameters is like recompiling a program every time.

91

CHAPTER 4: THE JOIN OPERATION

PIPELINING INTERMEDIATE RESULTS

Although intermediate results explain the algorithm very well, it does not mean that the database has to materialize it. That would mean storing the intermediate result of the first join before starting the next one. Instead, databases use pipelining to reduce memory usage. That means that each row from the intermediate result is immediately *pipelined* to the next join operation—avoiding the need to store the intermediate result set.

NESTED LOOPS

The nested loops join is the most fundamental join algorithm. It works like using two nested queries: the outer or driving query to fetch the results from one table and a second query *for each row* from the driving query to fetch the corresponding data from the other table.

You can actually use "nested selects" to implement the nested loops algorithm on your own. Nevertheless that is a troublesome approach because network latencies occur on top of disk latencies—making the overall response time even worse. "Nested selects" are still very common because it is easy to implement them without being aware of it. Object-relational mapping (ORM) tools are particularly "helpful" in this respect...to the extent that the so-called *N+1 selects problem* has gained a sad notoriety in the field.

The following examples show these "accidental nested select" joins produced with different ORM tools. The examples search for employees whose last name starts with 'WIN' and fetches all SALES for these employees.

The ORMs don't generate SQL joins—instead they query the SALES table with nested selects. This effect is known as the "N+1 selects problem" or shorter the "N+1 problem" because it executes N+1 selects in total if the driving query returns N rows.

92

NESTED LOOPS

JAVA

The JPA example uses the CriteriaBuilder interface.

```java
CriteriaBuilder queryBuilder = em.getCriteriaBuilder();
CriteriaQuery<Employees>
    query = queryBuilder.createQuery(Employees.class);
Root<Employees> r = query.from(Employees.class);
query.where(
  queryBuilder.like(
    queryBuilder.upper(r.get(Employees_.lastName)),
    "WIN%"
  )
);

List<Employees> emp = em.createQuery(query).getResultList();

for (Employees e: emp) {
  // process Employee
  for (Sales s: e.getSales()) {
    // process sale for Employee
  }
}
```

Hibernate JPA 3.6.0 generates N+1 **select** queries:

```
select employees0_.subsidiary_id as subsidiary1_0_
       -- MORE COLUMNS
  from employees employees0_
 where upper(employees0_.last_name) like ?

  select sales0_.subsidiary_id as subsidiary4_0_1_
         -- MORE COLUMNS
    from sales sales0_
   where sales0_.subsidiary_id=?
     and sales0_.employee_id=?

  select sales0_.subsidiary_id as subsidiary4_0_1_
         -- MORE COLUMNS
    from sales sales0_
   where sales0_.subsidiary_id=?
     and sales0_.employee_id=?
```

93

CHAPTER 4: THE JOIN OPERATION

PERL

The following sample demonstrates Perl's DBIx::Class framework:

```
my @employees =
    $schema->resultset('Employees')
            ->search({'UPPER(last_name)' => {-like=>'WIN%'}});

foreach my $employee (@employees) {
    # process Employee
    foreach my $sale ($employee->sales) {
        # process Sale for Employee
    }
}
```

DBIx::Class 0.08192 generates N+1 **select** queries:

```
SELECT me.employee_id, me.subsidiary_id
    , me.last_name, me.first_name, me.date_of_birth
  FROM employees me
 WHERE ( UPPER(last_name) LIKE ? )


    SELECT me.sale_id, me.employee_id, me.subsidiary_id
        , me.sale_date, me.eur_value
      FROM sales me
     WHERE ( ( me.employee_id = ?
       AND me.subsidiary_id = ? ) )

    SELECT me.sale_id, me.employee_id, me.subsidiary_id
        , me.sale_date, me.eur_value
      FROM sales me
     WHERE ( ( me.employee_id = ?
       AND me.subsidiary_id = ? ) )
```

PHP

The Doctrine sample uses the query builder interface:

```
$qb = $em->createQueryBuilder();
$qb->select('e')
    ->from('Employees', 'e')
    ->where("upper(e.last_name) like :last_name")
    ->setParameter('last_name', 'WIN%');
$r = $qb->getQuery()->getResult();

foreach ($r as $row) {
    // process Employee
    foreach ($row->getSales() as $sale) {
        // process Sale for Employee
    }
}
```

94

NESTED LOOPS

Doctrine 2.0.5 generates N+1 **select** queries:

```
SELECT e0_.employee_id AS employee_id0 -- MORE COLUMNS
  FROM employees e0_
 WHERE UPPER(e0_.last_name) LIKE ?

    SELECT t0.sale_id AS SALE_ID1 -- MORE COLUMNS
      FROM sales t0
     WHERE t0.subsidiary_id = ?
       AND t0.employee_id = ?

    SELECT t0.sale_id AS SALE_ID1 -- MORE COLUMNS
      FROM sales t0
     WHERE t0.subsidiary_id = ?
       AND t0.employee_id = ?
```

ENABLING SQL LOGGING

Enable SQL logging during development and review the generated SQL statements.

DBIx::CLASS
export `DBIC_TRACE=1` in your shell.

DOCTRINE
Only on source code level—don't forget to disable this for production. Consider building your own configurable logger.

```
$logger = new \Doctrine\DBAL\Logging\EchoSqlLogger;
$config->setSQLLogger($logger);
```

HIBERNATE (NATIVE)
`<property name="show_sql">true</property>` in `App.config` or `hibernate.cfg.xml`

JPA
In `persistence.xml` but depending on the JPA provider:

```
<property name="eclipselink.logging.level" value="FINE"/>
<property name="hibernate.show_sql" value="TRUE"/>
<property name="openjpa.Log" value="SQL=TRACE"/>
```

Most ORMs offer a programmatic way to enable SQL logging as well. That involves the risk of accidentally deploying the setting in production.

95

CHAPTER 4: THE JOIN OPERATION

Even though the "nested selects" approach is an anti-pattern, it still explains the *nested loops* join pretty well. The database executes the join exactly as the ORM tools above. Indexing for a nested loops join is therefore like indexing for the above shown **select** statements. That is a function-based index on the table EMPLOYEES and a concatenated index for the join predicates on the SALES table:

```
CREATE INDEX emp_up_name ON employees (UPPER(last_name));
CREATE INDEX sales_emp ON sales (subsidiary_id, employee_id);
```

An SQL join is still more efficient than the nested selects approach — even though it performs the same index lookups — because it avoids a lot of network communication. It is even faster if the total amount of transferred data is bigger because of the duplication of employee attributes for each sale. That is because of the two dimensions of performance: response time and throughput; in computer networks we call them *latency* and *bandwidth*. Bandwidth has only a minor impact on the response time but latencies have a huge impact. That means that the number of database round trips is more important for the response time than the amount of data transferred.

> **TIP**
>
> Execute joins in the database.

Most ORM tools offer some way to create SQL joins. The so-called *eager fetching* mode is probably the most important one. It is typically configured at the property level in the entity mappings — e.g., for the employees property in the Sales class. The ORM tool will then always join the EMPLOYEES table when accessing the SALES table. Configuring eager fetching in the entity mappings only makes sense if you always need the employee details along with the sales data.

Eager fetching is counterproductive if you do not need the child records every time you access the parent object. For a telephone directory application, it does not make sense to load the SALES records when showing employee details. You might need the related sales data in other cases — but not always. A static configuration is no solution.

For optimal performance, you need to gain full control over joins. The following examples show how to get the greatest flexibility by controlling the join behavior at runtime.

96

NESTED LOOPS

JAVA

The JPA CriteriaBuilder interface provides the Root<>.fetch() method for controlling joins. It allows you to specify when and how to join referred objects to the main query. In this example we use a left join to retrieve all employees even if some of them do not have sales.

> **WARNING**
>
> JPA and Hibernate return the employees *for each sale.*
>
> That means that an employee with 30 sales will appear 30 times. Although it is very disturbing, it is the specified behavior (EJB 3.0 persistency, paragraph 4.4.5.3 "Fetch Joins"). You can either manually de-duplicate the parent relation or use the function distinct() as shown in the example.

```java
CriteriaBuilder qb = em.getCriteriaBuilder();
CriteriaQuery<Employees> q = qb.createQuery(Employees.class);
Root<Employees> r = q.from(Employees.class);
q.where(queryBuilder.like(
    queryBuilder.upper(r.get(Employees_.lastName)),
    "WIN%")
);

r.fetch("sales", JoinType.LEFT);
// needed to avoid duplication of Employee records
query.distinct(true);

List<Employees> emp = em.createQuery(query).getResultList();
```

Hibernate 3.6.0 generates the following SQL statement:

```sql
select distinct
        employees0_.subsidiary_id as subsidiary1_0_0_
    , employees0_.employee_id as employee2_0_0_
    -- MORE COLUMNS
    , sales1_.sale_id as sale1_0__
  from employees employees0_
  left outer join sales sales1_
        on employees0_.subsidiary_id=sales1_.subsidiary_id
        and employees0_.employee_id=sales1_.employee_id
 where upper(employees0_.last_name) like ?
```

The query has the expected left join but also an unnecessary distinct keyword. Unfortunately, JPA does not provide separate API calls to filter duplicated parent entries without de-duplicating the child records as

97

well. The distinct keyword in the SQL query is alarming because most databases will actually filter duplicate records. Only a few databases recognize that the primary keys guarantees uniqueness in that case anyway.

The native Hibernate API solves the problem on the client side using a result set transformer:

```
Criteria c = session.createCriteria(Employees.class);
c.add(Restrictions.ilike("lastName", 'Win%'));

c.setFetchMode("sales", FetchMode.JOIN);
c.setResultTransformer(Criteria.DISTINCT_ROOT_ENTITY);

List<Employees> result = c.list();
```

It generates the following query:

```
select this_.subsidiary_id as subsidiary1_0_1_
     , this_.employee_id as employee2_0_1_
       -- MORE this_ columns on employees
     , sales2_.sale_id as sale1_3_
       -- MORE sales2_ columns on sales
  from employees this_
  left outer join sales sales2_
         on this_.subsidiary_id=sales2_.subsidiary_id
        and this_.employee_id=sales2_.employee_id
 where lower(this_.last_name) like ?
```

This method produces straight SQL without unintended clauses. Note that Hibernate uses lower() for case-insensitive queries—an important detail for function-based indexing.

PERL

The following example uses Perl's DBIx::Class framework:

```
my @employees =
    $schema->resultset('Employees')
            ->search({ 'UPPER(last_name)' => {-like => 'WIN%'}
                     , {prefetch => ['sales']}
                     });
```

DBIx::Class 0.08192 generates the following SQL statement:

```
SELECT me.employee_id, me.subsidiary_id, me.last_name
       -- MORE COLUMNS
  FROM employees me
  LEFT JOIN sales sales
        ON (sales.employee_id   = me.employee_id
       AND  sales.subsidiary_id = me.subsidiary_id)
 WHERE ( UPPER(last_name) LIKE ? )
 ORDER BY sales.employee_id, sales.subsidiary_id
```

Note the **order by** clause—it was not requested by the application. The database has to sort the result set accordingly, and that might take a while.

PHP

The following example uses PHP's Doctrine framework:

```
$qb = $em->createQueryBuilder();
$qb->select('e,s')
    ->from('Employees', 'e')
    ->leftJoin('e.sales', 's')
    ->where("upper(e.last_name) like :last_name")
    ->setParameter('last_name', 'WIN%');
$r = $qb->getQuery()->getResult();
```

Doctrine 2.0.5 generates the following SQL statement:

```
SELECT e0_.employee_id AS employee_id0
       -- MORE COLUMNS
  FROM employees e0_
  LEFT JOIN sales s1_
        ON e0_.subsidiary_id = s1_.subsidiary_id
       AND e0_.employee_id = s1_.employee_id
 WHERE UPPER(e0_.last_name) LIKE ?
```

CHAPTER 4: THE JOIN OPERATION

The execution plan shows the NESTED LOOPS OUTER operation:

```
-----------------------------------------------------------------
|Id |Operation                       | Name         | Rows | Cost |
-----------------------------------------------------------------
| 0 |SELECT STATEMENT                |              | 822  | 38   |
| 1 | NESTED LOOPS OUTER             |              | 822  | 38   |
| 2 |  TABLE ACCESS BY INDEX ROWID| EMPLOYEES    | 1    | 4    |
|*3 |   INDEX RANGE SCAN             | EMP_UP_NAME  | 1    |      |
| 4 |  TABLE ACCESS BY INDEX ROWID| SALES        | 821  | 34   |
|*5 |   INDEX RANGE SCAN             | SALES_EMP    | 31   |      |
-----------------------------------------------------------------

Predicate Information (identified by operation id):
---------------------------------------------------
  3 - access(UPPER("LAST_NAME") LIKE 'WIN%')
      filter(UPPER("LAST_NAME") LIKE 'WIN%')
  5 - access("E0_"."SUBSIDIARY_ID"="S1_"."SUBSIDIARY_ID"(+)
        AND  "E0_"."EMPLOYEE_ID"  ="S1_"."EMPLOYEE_ID"(+))
```

The database retrieves the result from the EMPLOYEES table via EMP_UP_NAME first and fetches the corresponding records from the SALES table for each employee afterwards.

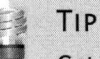

TIP

Get to know your ORM and take control of joins.

The nested loops join delivers good performance if the driving query returns a small result set. Otherwise, the optimizer might choose an entirely different join algorithm—like the hash join described in the next section, but this is only possible if the application uses a join to tell the database what data it actually needs.

Hash Join

The hash join algorithm aims for the weak spot of the nested loops join: the many B-tree traversals when executing the inner query. Instead it loads the candidate records from one side of the join into a hash table that can be probed very quickly for each row from the other side of the join. Tuning a hash join requires an entirely different indexing approach than the nested loops join. Beyond that, it is also possible to improve hash join performance by selecting fewer *columns* — a challenge for most ORM tools.

The indexing strategy for a hash join is very different because there is no need to index the join columns. Only indexes for *independent* **where** predicates improve hash join performance.

> **TIP**
>
> Index the *independent* **where** predicates to improve hash join performance.

Consider the following example. It selects all sales for the past six months with the corresponding employee details:

```
SELECT *
  FROM sales s
  JOIN employees e ON (s.subsidiary_id = e.subsidiary_id
                   AND s.employee_id   = e.employee_id  )
 WHERE s.sale_date > trunc(sysdate) - INTERVAL '6' MONTH
```

The SALE_DATE filter is the only independent **where** clause — that means it refers to one table only and does not belong to the join predicates.

CHAPTER 4: THE JOIN OPERATION

```
--------------------------------------------------------------
| Id | Operation           | Name      | Rows  | Bytes | Cost |
--------------------------------------------------------------
|  0 | SELECT STATEMENT    |           | 49244 |   59M| 12049|
|* 1 |  HASH JOIN          |           | 49244 |   59M| 12049|
|  2 |   TABLE ACCESS FULL| EMPLOYEES | 10000 |    9M|   478|
|* 3 |   TABLE ACCESS FULL| SALES     | 49244 |   10M| 10521|
--------------------------------------------------------------

Predicate Information (identified by operation id):
--------------------------------------------------------------
   1 - access("S"."SUBSIDIARY_ID"="E"."SUBSIDIARY_ID"
          AND "S"."EMPLOYEE_ID"  ="E"."EMPLOYEE_ID")
   3 - filter("S"."SALE_DATE">TRUNC(SYSDATE@!)
                       -INTERVAL'+00-06' YEAR(2) TO MONTH)
```

The first execution step is a full table scan to load all employees into a hash table (plan id 2). The hash table uses the join predicates as key. In the next step, the database does another full table scan on the SALES table and discards all sales that do not satisfy the condition on SALE_DATE (plan id 3). For the remaining SALES records, the database accesses the hash table to load the corresponding employee details.

The sole purpose of the hash table is to act as a temporary in-memory structure to avoid accessing the EMPLOYEE table many times. The hash table is initially loaded in one shot so that there is no need for an index to efficiently fetch single records. The predicate information confirms that not a single filter is applied on the EMPLOYEES table (plan id 2). The query doesn't have any independent predicates on this table.

> **IMPORTANT**
> Indexing join predicates doesn't improve hash join performance.

That does not mean it is impossible to index a hash join. The independent predicates can be indexed. These are the conditions which are applied during one of the two table access operations. In the above example, it is the filter on SALE_DATE.

```
CREATE INDEX sales_date ON sales (sale_date);
```

The following execution plan uses this index. Nevertheless it uses a full table scan for the EMPLOYEES table because the query has no independent **where** predicate on EMPLOYEES.

102

HASH JOIN

```
-----------------------------------------------------------------
| Id | Operation                   | Name      | Bytes| Cost|
-----------------------------------------------------------------
|  0 | SELECT STATEMENT            |           |  59M| 3252|
|* 1 |  HASH JOIN                  |           |  59M| 3252|
|  2 |   TABLE ACCESS FULL         | EMPLOYEES |   9M|  478|
|  3 |   TABLE ACCESS BY INDEX ROWID| SALES    |  10M| 1724|
|* 4 |    INDEX RANGE SCAN         | SALES_DATE|     |     |
-----------------------------------------------------------------

Predicate Information (identified by operation id):
---------------------------------------------------
   1 - access("S"."SUBSIDIARY_ID"="E"."SUBSIDIARY_ID"
           AND "S"."EMPLOYEE_ID"  ="E"."EMPLOYEE_ID"  )
   4 - access("S"."SALE_DATE" > TRUNC(SYSDATE@!)
                        -INTERVAL'+00-06' YEAR(2) TO MONTH)
```

Indexing a hash join is—contrary to the nested loops join—symmetric. That means that the join order does not influence indexing. The SALES_DATE index can be used to load the hash table if the join order is reversed.

> **NOTE**
>
> Indexing a hash join is independent of the join order.

A rather different approach to optimizing hash join performance is to minimize the hash table size. This method works because an optimal hash join is only possible if the entire hash table fits into memory. The optimizer will therefore automatically use the smaller side of the join for the hash table. The Oracle execution plan shows the estimated memory requirement in the "Bytes" column. In the above execution plan, the EMPLOYEES table needs nine megabytes and is thus the smaller one.

It is also possible to reduce the hash table size by changing the SQL query, for example by adding extra conditions so that the database loads fewer candidate records into the hash table. Continuing the above example it would mean adding a filter on the DEPARTMENT attribute so only sales staff is considered. This improves hash join performance even if there is no index on the DEPARTMENT attribute because the database does not need to store employees who cannot have sales in the hash table. When doing so you have to make sure there are no SALES records for employees that do not work in the respective department. Use constraints to guard your assumptions.

CHAPTER 4: THE JOIN OPERATION

When minimizing the hash table size, the relevant factor is not the number of rows but the memory footprint. It is, in fact, also possible to reduce the hash table size by selecting fewer *columns*—only the attributes you really need:

```
SELECT s.sale_date, s.eur_value
     , e.last_name, e.first_name
  FROM sales s
  JOIN employees e ON (s.subsidiary_id = e.subsidiary_id
                   AND s.employee_id   = e.employee_id  )
 WHERE s.sale_date > trunc(sysdate) - INTERVAL '6' MONTH
```

That method seldom introduces bugs because dropping the wrong column will probably quickly result in an error message. Nevertheless it is possible to cut the hash table size considerably, in this particular case from 9 megabyte down to 234 kilobytes—a reduction of 97%.

```
---------------------------------------------------------------
| Id | Operation                    | Name       | Bytes| Cost|
---------------------------------------------------------------
|  0 | SELECT STATEMENT             |            | 2067K| 2202|
|* 1 |  HASH JOIN                   |            | 2067K| 2202|
|  2 |   TABLE ACCESS FULL          | EMPLOYEES  |  234K|  478|
|  3 |   TABLE ACCESS BY INDEX ROWID| SALES      |  913K| 1724|
|* 4 |    INDEX RANGE SCAN          | SALES_DATE |      |  133|
---------------------------------------------------------------
```

> **TIP**
>
> Select fewer columns to improve hash join performance.

Although at first glance it seems simple to remove a few columns from an SQL statement, it is a real challenge when using an object-relational mapping (ORM) tool. Support for so-called *partial objects* is very sparse. The following examples show some possibilities.

JAVA

JPA defines the FetchType.LAZY in the @Basic annotation. It can be applied on property level:

```
@Column(name="junk")
@Basic(fetch=FetchType.LAZY)
private String junk;
```

104

JPA providers are free to ignore it:

> The LAZY strategy is a hint to the persistence provider runtime that data should be fetched lazily when it is first accessed. The implementation is permitted to eagerly fetch data for which the LAZY strategy hint has been specified.
>
> —EJB 3.0 JPA, paragraph 9.1.18

Hibernate 3.6 implements lazy property fetching via compile time bytecode instrumentation. The instrumentation adds extra code to the compiled classes that does not fetch the LAZY properties until accessed. The approach is fully transparent to the application but it opens the door to a new dimension of N+1 problems: one **select** for each record *and property*. This is particularly dangerous because JPA does not offer runtime control to fetch eagerly if needed.

Hibernate's native query language HQL solves the problem with the FETCH ALL PROPERTIES clause:

```
select s from Sales s FETCH ALL PROPERTIES
  inner join fetch s.employee e FETCH ALL PROPERTIES
  where s.saleDate >:dt
```

The FETCH ALL PROPERTIES clause forces Hibernate to eagerly fetch the entity—even when using instrumented code and the LAZY annotation.

Another option for loading only selected columns is to use data transport objects (DTOs) instead of entities. This method works the same way in HQL and JPQL, that is you initialize an object in the query:

```
select new SalesHeadDTO(s.saleDate , s.eurValue
                        ,e.firstName, e.lastName)
  from Sales s
  join s.employee e
 where s.saleDate > :dt
```

The query selects the requested data only and returns a SalesHeadDTO object—a simple Java object (POJO), not an entity.

Chapter 4: The Join Operation

PERL

The DBIx::Class framework does not act as entity manager so that inheritance doesn't cause aliasing problems[1]. The cookbook supports this approach. The following schema definition defines the Sales class on two levels:

```perl
package UseTheIndexLuke::Schema::Result::SalesHead;
use base qw/DBIx::Class::Core/;

__PACKAGE__->table('sales');
__PACKAGE__->add_columns(qw/sale_id employee_id subsidiary_id
                            sale_date eur_value/);
__PACKAGE__->set_primary_key(qw/sale_id/);
__PACKAGE__->belongs_to('employee', 'Employees',
           {'foreign.employee_id'   => 'self.employee_id'
           ,'foreign.subsidiary_id' => 'self.subsidiary_id'});

package UseTheIndexLuke::Schema::Result::Sales;
use base qw/UseTheIndexLuke::Schema::Result::SalesHead/;

__PACKAGE__->table('sales');
__PACKAGE__->add_columns(qw/junk/);
```

The Sales class is derived from the SalesHead class and adds the missing attribute. You can use both classes as you need them. Please note that the table setup is required in the derived class as well.

You can fetch all employee details via prefetch or just selected columns as shown below:

```perl
my @sales =
    $schema->resultset('SalesHead')
           ->search($cond
                   ,{       join => 'employee'
                    ,'+columns' => ['employee.first_name'
                                   ,'employee.last_name']
                    }
                   );
```

It is not possible to load only selected columns from the root table— SalesHead in this case.

---

[1] http://en.wikipedia.org/wiki/Aliasing_%28computing%29

106

HASH JOIN

DBIx::Class 0.08192 generates the following SQL. It fetches all columns from the SALES table and the selected attributes from EMPLOYEES:

```
SELECT me.sale_id,
       me.employee_id,
       me.subsidiary_id,
       me.sale_date,
       me.eur_value,
       employee.first_name,
       employee.last_name
  FROM sales me
  JOIN employees employee
       ON( employee.employee_id   = me.employee_id
       AND  employee.subsidiary_id = me.subsidiary_id)
 WHERE(sale_date > ?)
```

PHP

Version 2 of the Doctrine framework supports attribute selection at runtime. The documentation states that the partially loaded objects might behave oddly and requires the **partial** keyword to acknowledge the risks. Furthermore, you must select the primary key columns explicitly:

```
$qb = $em->createQueryBuilder();
$qb->select('partial s.{sale_id, sale_date, eur_value},'
     . 'partial e.{employee_id, subsidiary_id, '
            . 'first_name , last_name}')
  ->from('Sales', 's')
  ->join('s.employee', 'e')
  ->where("s.sale_date > :dt")
  ->setParameter('dt', $dt, Type::DATETIME);
```

The generated SQL contains the requested columns and once more the SUBSIDIARY_ID and EMPLOYEE_ID from the SALES table.

107

CHAPTER 4: THE JOIN OPERATION

```sql
SELECT s0_.sale_id       AS sale_id0,
       s0_.sale_date     AS sale_date1,
       s0_.eur_value     AS eur_value2,
       e1_.employee_id   AS employee_id3,
       e1_.subsidiary_id AS subsidiary_id4,
       e1_.first_name    AS first_name5,
       e1_.last_name     AS last_name6,
       s0_.subsidiary_id AS subsidiary_id7,
       s0_.employee_id   AS employee_id8
  FROM sales s0_
  INNER JOIN employees e1_
        ON s0_.subsidiary_id = e1_.subsidiary_id
        AND s0_.employee_id  = e1_.employee_id
  WHERE s0_.sale_date > ?
```

The returned objects are compatible with fully loaded objects, but the missing columns remain uninitialized. Accessing them does *not* trigger an exception.

WARNING

MySQL does not support hash joins at all (feature request #59025)

Sort Merge

The sort-merge join combines two sorted lists like a zipper. Both sides of the join must be sorted by the join predicates.

A sort-merge join needs the same indexes as the hash join, that is an index for the independent conditions to read all candidate records in one shot. Indexing the join predicates is useless. Everything is just like a hash join so far. Nevertheless there is one aspect that is unique to the sort-merge join: absolute symmetry. The join order does not make any difference—not even for performance. This property is very useful for outer joins. For other algorithms the direction of the outer joins (left or right) implies the join order—but not for the sort-merge join. The sort-merge join can even do a left and right outer join at the same time—a so-called full outer join.

Although the sort-merge join performs very well once the inputs are sorted, it is hardly used because sorting both sides is very expensive. The hash join, on the other hand, needs to preprocess only one side.

The strength of the sort-merge join emerges if the inputs are already sorted. This is possible by exploiting the index order to avoid the sort operations entirely. Chapter 6, *"Sorting and Grouping"*, explains this concept in detail. The hash join algorithm is superior in many cases nevertheless.

CHAPTER 5

CLUSTERING DATA

THE SECOND POWER OF INDEXING

The term *cluster* is used in various fields. A star cluster, for example, is a group of stars. A computer cluster, on the other hand, is a group of computers that work closely together—either to solve a complex problem (high-performance computing cluster) or to increase availability (failover cluster). Generally speaking, clusters are related things that appear together.

In the field of computing there is one more type of cluster—one that is often misunderstood: the data cluster. Clustering data means to store consecutively accessed data closely together so that accessing it requires fewer IO operations. Data clusters are very important in terms of database tuning. Computer clusters, on the other hand, are also very common in a database context—thus making the term *cluster* very ambiguous. The sentence "Let's use a cluster to improve database performance" is just one example; it might refer to a computer cluster but could also mean a data cluster. In this chapter, cluster generally refers to *data clusters*.

The simplest data cluster in an SQL database is the row. Databases store all columns of a row in the same database block if possible. Exceptions apply if a row doesn't fit into a single block—e.g., when LOB types are involved.

COLUMN STORES

Column oriented databases, or column-stores, organize tables in a columned way. This model is beneficial when accessing many rows but only a few columns—a pattern that is very common in data warehouses (OLAP).

111

CHAPTER 5: CLUSTERING DATA

Indexes allow one to cluster data. The basis for this was already explained in Chapter 1, *"Anatomy of an Index"*: the index leaf nodes store the indexed columns in an ordered fashion so that similar values are stored next to each other. That means that indexes build clusters of rows with similar values. This capability to cluster data is so important that I refer to it as the *second power of indexing*.

The following sections explain how to use indexes to cluster data and improve query performance.

INDEX FILTER PREDICATES USED INTENTIONALLY

Very often index filter predicates indicate improper index usage caused by an incorrect column order in a concatenated index. Nevertheless index filter predicates can be used for a good reason as well—not to improve range scan performance but to group consecutively accessed data together.

Where clause predicates that cannot serve as access predicate are good candidates for this technique:

```
SELECT first_name, last_name, subsidiary_id, phone_number
  FROM employees
 WHERE subsidiary_id = ?
   AND UPPER(last_name) LIKE '%INA%';
```

Remember that LIKE expressions with leading wildcards cannot use the index tree. That means that indexing LAST_NAME doesn't narrow the scanned index range—no matter if you index LAST_NAME or UPPER(last_name). This condition is therefore no good candidate for indexing.

However the condition on SUBSIDIARY_ID is well suited for indexing. We don't even need to add a new index because the SUBSIDIARY_ID is already the leading column in the index for the primary key.

112

INDEX FILTER PREDICATES USED INTENTIONALLY

```
-------------------------------------------------------------
|Id | Operation                   | Name        | Rows | Cost |
-------------------------------------------------------------
| 0 | SELECT STATEMENT            |             |   17 |  230 |
|*1 |   TABLE ACCESS BY INDEX ROWID| EMPLOYEES  |   17 |  230 |
|*2 |     INDEX RANGE SCAN        | EMPLOYEE_PK |  333 |    2 |
-------------------------------------------------------------

Predicate Information (identified by operation id):
---------------------------------------------------
   1 - filter(UPPER("LAST_NAME") LIKE '%INA%')
   2 - access("SUBSIDIARY_ID"=TO_NUMBER(:A))
```

In the above execution plan, the cost value raises a hundred times from the INDEX RANGE SCAN to the subsequent TABLE ACCESS BY INDEX ROWID operation. In other words: the table access causes the most work. It is actually a common pattern and is not a problem by itself. Nevertheless, it is the most significant contributor to the overall execution time of this query.

The table access is not necessarily a bottleneck if the accessed rows are stored in a single table block because the database can fetch all rows with a single read operation. If the same rows are spread across many different blocks, in contrast, the table access can become a serious performance problem because the database has to fetch many blocks in order to retrieve all the rows. That means the performance depends on the physical distribution of the accessed rows—in other words: it depends on the clustering of rows.

> **NOTE**
>
> The correlation between index order and table order is a performance benchmark—the so-called *index clustering factor.*

It is in fact possible to improve query performance by re-ordering the rows in the table so they correspond to the index order. This method is, however, rarely applicable because you can only store the table rows in one sequence. That means you can optimize the table for one index only. Even if you can choose a single index for which you would like to optimizer the table, it is still a difficult task because most databases only offer rudimentary tools for this task. So-called *row sequencing* is, after all, a rather impractical approach.

113

CHAPTER 5: CLUSTERING DATA

THE INDEX CLUSTERING FACTOR

The index clustering factor is an indirect measure of the probability that two succeeding index entries refer to the same table block. The optimizer takes this probability into account when calculating the cost value of the TABLE ACCESS BY INDEX ROWID operation.

This is exactly where the *second power of indexing*—clustering data—comes in. You can add many columns to an index so that they are automatically stored in a well defined order. That makes an index a powerful yet simple tool for clustering data.

To apply this concept to the above query, we must extend the index to cover all columns from the **where** clause—even if they do not narrow the scanned index range:

```
CREATE INDEX empsubupnam ON employees
       (subsidiary_id, UPPER(last_name));
```

The column SUBSIDIARY_ID is the first index column so it can be used as an access predicate. The expression UPPER(last_name) covers the LIKE filter as *index filter predicate*. Indexing the uppercase representation saves a few CPU cycles during execution, but a straight index on LAST_NAME would work as well. You'll find more about this in the next section.

```
---------------------------------------------------------------
|Id | Operation                   | Name        | Rows | Cost |
---------------------------------------------------------------
| 0 | SELECT STATEMENT            |             |   17 |   20 |
| 1 |  TABLE ACCESS BY INDEX ROWID| EMPLOYEES   |   17 |   20 |
|*2 |   INDEX RANGE SCAN          | EMPSUBUPNAM |   17 |    3 |
---------------------------------------------------------------

Predicate Information (identified by operation id):
---------------------------------------------------------------
   2 - access("SUBSIDIARY_ID"=TO_NUMBER(:A))
       filter(UPPER("LAST_NAME") LIKE '%INA%')
```

The new execution plan shows the very same operations as before. The cost value dropped considerably nonetheless. In the predicate information we can see that the LIKE filter is already applied during the INDEX RANGE SCAN. Rows that do not fulfill the LIKE filter are immediately discarded. The table access does not have any filter predicates anymore. That means it does not load rows that do not fulfill the **where** clause.

114

Index Filter Predicates Used Intentionally

The difference between the two execution plans is clearly visible in the "Rows" column. According to the optimizer's estimate, the query ultimately matches 17 records. The index scan in the first execution plan delivers 333 rows nevertheless. The database must then load these 333 rows from the table to apply the LIKE filter which reduces the result to 17 rows. In the second execution plan, the index access does not deliver those rows in the first place so the database needs to execute the TABLE ACCESS BY INDEX ROWID operation only 17 times.

You should also note that the cost value of the INDEX RANGE SCAN operation grew from two to three because the additional column makes the index bigger. In view of the performance gain, it is an acceptable compromise.

> **WARNING**
>
> Don't introduce a new index for the sole purpose of filter predicates. Extend an existing index instead and keep the maintenance effort low. With some databases you can even add columns to the index for the primary key that are not part of the primary key.

This trivial example seems to confirm the common wisdom to index every column from the where clause. This "wisdom", however, ignores the relevance of the column order which determines what conditions can be used as access predicates and thus has a huge impact on performance. The decision about column order should therefore never be left to chance.

The index size grows with the number of columns as well—especially when adding text columns. Of course the performance does not get better for a bigger index even though the logarithmic scalability limits the impact considerably. You should by no means add all columns that are mentioned in the where clause to an index but instead only use index filter predicates intentionally to reduce the data volume during an earlier execution step.

Index-Only Scan

The index-only scan is one of the most powerful tuning methods of all. It not only avoids accessing the table to evaluate the **where** clause, but avoids accessing the table completely if the database can find the selected columns in the index itself.

To cover an entire query, an index must contain *all* columns from the SQL statement—in particular also the columns from the **select** clause as shown in the following example:

```
CREATE INDEX sales_sub_eur
    ON sales
     ( subsidiary_id, eur_value );
SELECT SUM(eur_value)
  FROM sales
 WHERE subsidiary_id = ?;
```

Of course indexing the **where** clause takes precedence over the other clauses. The column SUBSIDIARY_ID is therefore in the first position so it qualifies as an access predicate.

The execution plan shows the index scan without a subsequent table access (TABLE ACCESS BY INDEX ROWID).

```
---------------------------------------------------------------
| Id  | Operation         | Name          | Rows  | Cost |
---------------------------------------------------------------
|   0 | SELECT STATEMENT  |               |     1 |  104 |
|   1 |  SORT AGGREGATE   |               |     1 |      |
|*  2 |   INDEX RANGE SCAN| SALES_SUB_EUR | 40388 |  104 |
---------------------------------------------------------------

Predicate Information (identified by operation id):
---------------------------------------------------------------
   2 - access("SUBSIDIARY_ID"=TO_NUMBER(:A))
```

The index covers the entire query so it is also called a *covering index*.

116

INDEX-ONLY SCAN

> **NOTE**
>
> If an index prevents a table access it is also called a *covering index*.
>
> The term is misleading, however, because it sounds like an index property. The phrase index-only scan correctly suggests that it is an execution plan operation.

The index has a copy of the EUR_VALUE column so the database can use the value stored in the index. Accessing the table is not required because the index has all of the information to satisfy the query.

An index-only scan can improve performance enormously. Just look at the row count estimate in the execution plan: the optimizer expects to aggregate more than 40,000 rows. That means that the index-only scan prevents 40,000 table fetches—if each row is in a different table block. If the index has a good clustering factor—that is, if the respective rows are well clustered in a few table blocks—the advantage may be significantly lower.

Besides the clustering factor, the number of selected rows limits the potential performance gain of an index-only scan. If you select a single row, for example, you can only save a single table access. Considering that the tree traversal needs to fetch a few blocks as well, the saved table access might become negligible.

> **IMPORTANT**
>
> The performance advantage of an index-only scans depends on the number of accessed rows and the index clustering factor.

The index-only scan is an aggressive indexing strategy. Do not design an index for an index-only scan on suspicion only because it unnecessarily uses memory and increases the maintenance effort needed for **update** statements. See Chapter 8, *"Modifying Data"*. In practice, you should first index without considering the **select** clause and only extend the index if needed.

117

CHAPTER 5: CLUSTERING DATA

Index-only scans can also cause unpleasant surprises, for example if we limit the query to recent sales:

```
SELECT SUM(eur_value)
  FROM sales
 WHERE subsidiary_id = ?
   AND sale_date > ?;
```

Without looking at the execution plan, one could expect the query to run faster because it selects fewer rows. The where clause, however, refers to a column that is not in the index so that the database must access the table to load this column.

```
-----------------------------------------------------------
|Id | Operation                   | Name      | Rows  |Cost |
-----------------------------------------------------------
| 0 | SELECT STATEMENT            |           |     1 | 371 |
| 1 |  SORT AGGREGATE             |           |     1 |     |
|*2 |   TABLE ACCESS BY INDEX ROWID| SALES     |  2019 | 371 |
|*3 |    INDEX RANGE SCAN         | SALES_DATE| 10541 |  30 |
-----------------------------------------------------------

Predicate Information (identified by operation id):
---------------------------------------------------
   2 - filter("SUBSIDIARY_ID"=TO_NUMBER(:A))
   3 - access("SALE_DATE">:B)
```

The table access increases the response time although the query selects fewer rows. The relevant factor is not how many rows the query delivers but how many rows the database must inspect to find them.

WARNING

Extending the where clause can cause "illogical" performance behavior. Check the execution plan before extending queries.

If an index can no longer be used for an index-only scan, the optimizer will choose the next best execution plan. That means the optimizer might select an entirely different execution plan or, as above, a similar execution plan with another index. In this case it uses an index on SALE_DATE, which is a leftover from the previous chapter.

118

INDEX-ONLY SCAN

From the optimizer's perspective, this index has two advantages over SALES_SUB_EUR. The optimizer believes that the filter on SALE_DATE is more selective than the one on SUBSIDIARY_ID. You can see that in the respective "Rows" column of the last two execution plans (about 10,000 versus 40,000). These estimations are, however, purely arbitrary because the query uses bind parameters. The SALE_DATE condition could, for example, select the entire table when providing the date of the first sale.

The second advantage of the SALES_DATE index is that is has a better clustering factor. This is a valid reason because the SALES table only grows chronologically. New rows are always appended to the end of the table as long as there are no rows deleted. The table order therefore corresponds to the index order because both are roughly sorted chronologically—the index has a good clustering factor.

When using an index with a good clustering factor, the selected tables rows are stored closely together so that the database only needs to read a few table blocks to get all the rows. Using this index, the query might be fast enough without an index-only scan. In this case we should remove the unneeded columns from the other index again.

> **NOTE**
>
> Some indexes have a good clustering factor automatically so that the performance advantage of an index-only scan is minimal.

In this particular example, there was a happy coincidence. The new filter on SALE_DATE not only prevented an index-only scan but also opened a new access path at the same time. The optimizer was therefore able to limit the performance impact of this change. It is, however, also possible to prevent an index only scan by adding columns to other clauses. However adding a column to the **select** clause can never open a new access path which could limit the impact of losing the index-only scan.

> **TIP**
>
> Maintain your index-only scans.
>
> Add comments that remind you about an index-only scan and refer to that page so anyone can read about it.

CHAPTER 5: CLUSTERING DATA

Function-based indexes can also cause unpleasant surprises in connection with index-only scans. An index on UPPER(last_name) cannot be used for an index-only scan when selecting the LAST_NAME column. In the previous section we should have indexed the LAST_NAME column itself to support the LIKE filter and allow it to be used for an index-only scan when selecting the LAST_NAME column.

> **TIP**
>
> Always aim to index the original data as that is often the most useful information you can put into an index.
>
> Avoid function-based indexing for expressions that cannot be used as access predicates.

Aggregating queries like the one shown above make good candidates for index-only scans. They query many rows but only a few columns, making a slim index sufficient for supporting an index-only scan. The more columns you query, the more columns you have to add to the indexed to support an index-only scan. As a developer you should therefore only select the columns you really need.

> **TIP**
>
> Avoid **select** * and fetch only the columns you need.

Regardless of the fact that indexing many rows needs a lot of space, you can also reach the limits of your database. Most databases impose rather rigid limits on the number of columns per index and the total size of an index entry. That means you cannot index an arbitrary number of columns nor arbitrarily long columns. The following overview lists the most important limitations. Nevertheless there are indexes that cover an entire table as we see in the next section.

> **THINK ABOUT IT**
>
> Queries that do not select any table columns are often executed with index-only scans.
>
> Can you think of a meaningful example?

120

INDEX-ONLY SCAN

MySQL

MySQL 5.6 with InnoDB limits every single column to 767 bytes and all columns together to 3072 bytes. MyISAM indexes are limited to 16 columns and a maximum key length of 1000 bytes.

MySQL has a unique feature called "prefix indexing" (sometimes also called "partial indexing"). This means indexing only the first few characters of a column—so it has nothing to do with the partial indexes described in Chapter 2. If you index a column that exceeds the allowed column length (767 bytes for InnoDB), MySQL automatically truncates the column accordingly. This is the reason the create index statement succeeds with the warning "Specified key was too long; max key length is 767 bytes" if you exceed the limit. That means that the index doesn't contain a full copy of the column anymore and is therefore of limited use for an index-only scan (similar to a function-based index).

You can use MySQL's prefix indexing explicitly to prevent exceeding the total key length limit if you get the error message "Specified key was too long; max key length is [1000/3072] bytes." The following example only indexes the first ten characters of the LAST_NAME column.

```
CREATE INDEX .. ON employees (last_name(10));
```

Oracle Database

The maximum index key length depends on the block size and the index storage parameters (75% of the database block size minus some overhead). A B-tree index is limited to 32 columns.

When using Oracle 11g with all defaults in place (8k blocks), the maximum index key length is 6398 bytes. Exceeding this limit causes the error message "ORA-01450: maximum key length (6398) exceeded."

PostgreSQL

The PostgreSQL database supports index-only scans since release 9.2.

The key length of B-tree indexes is limited to 2713 bytes (hardcoded, approx. BLCKSZ/3). The respective error message *"index row size ... exceeds btree maximum, 2713"* appears only when executing an **insert** or **update** that exceeds the limit. B-tree indexes can contain up to 32 columns.

CHAPTER 5: CLUSTERING DATA

SQL SERVER
Since version 2016, SQL Server supports up to 32 key columns. The total length limit is 1700 Bytes (900 Bytes for clustered indexes).[1] Nevertheless, SQL Server has a feature that allows you to add arbitrarily long columns to an index for the sole purpose of supporting an index-only scan. For that, SQL Server distinguishes between key columns and nonkey columns.

Key columns are index columns as they were discussed so far. Nonkey columns are additional columns that are only stored in the index leaf nodes. Nonkey columns can be arbitrarily long but cannot be used as access predicates (seek predicates).

Nonkey columns are defined with the **include** keyword of the **create index** command:

```
CREATE INDEX empsubupnam
    ON employees
        (subsidiary_id, last_name)
INCLUDE(phone_number, first_name);
```

INDEX-ORGANIZED TABLES

The index-only scan executes an SQL statement using only the redundant data stored in the index. The original data in the heap table is not needed. If we take that concept to the next level and put all columns into the index, you may wonder why we need the heap table.

Some databases can indeed use an index as primary table store. The Oracle database calls this concept *index-organized tables (IOT)*, other databases use the term *clustered index*. In this section, both terms are used to either put the emphasis on the table or the index characteristics as needed.

An index-organized table is thus a B-tree index without a heap table. This results in two benefits: (1) it saves the space for the heap structure; (2) every access on a clustered index is automatically an index-only scan. Both benefits sound promising but are hardly achievable in practice.

Before SQL Server 2016: 16 columns and 900 bytes.

INDEX-ORGANIZED TABLES

The drawbacks of an index-organized table become apparent when creating another index on the same table. Analogous to a regular index, a so-called *secondary index* refers to the original table data—which is stored in the clustered index. There, the data is not stored statically as in a heap table but can move at any time to maintain the index order. It is therefore not possible to store the physical location of the rows in the index-organized table in the secondary index. The database must use a logical key instead.

The following figures show an index lookup for finding all sales on May 23rd 2012. For comparison, we will first look at Figure 5.1 that shows the process when using a heap table. The execution involves two steps: (1) the INDEX RANGE SCAN; (2) the TABLE ACCESS BY INDEX ROWID.

Figure 5.1. Index-Based Access on a Heap Table

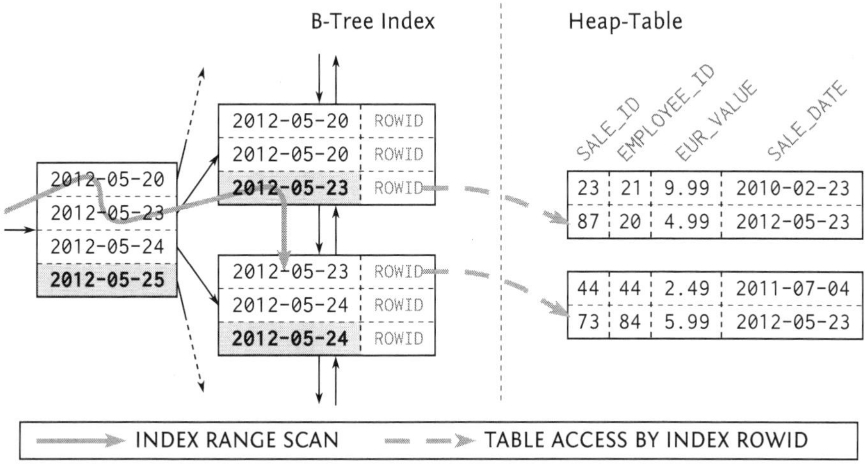

Although the table access might become a bottleneck, it is still limited to one read operation per row because the index has the ROWID as a direct pointer to the table row. The database can immediately load the row from the heap table because the index has its exact position. The picture changes, however, when using a secondary index on an index-organized table. A secondary index does not store a physical pointer (ROWID) but only the key values of the clustered index—the so-called *clustering key*. Often that is the primary key of the index-organized table.

123

CHAPTER 5: CLUSTERING DATA

Accessing a secondary index does not deliver a ROWID but a logical key for searching the clustered index. A single access, however, is not sufficient for searching clustered index—it requires a full tree traversal. That means that accessing a table via a secondary index searches two indexes: the secondary index once (INDEX RANGE SCAN), then the clustered index *for each row* found in the secondary index (INDEX UNIQUE SCAN).

Figure 5.2. Secondary Index on an IOT

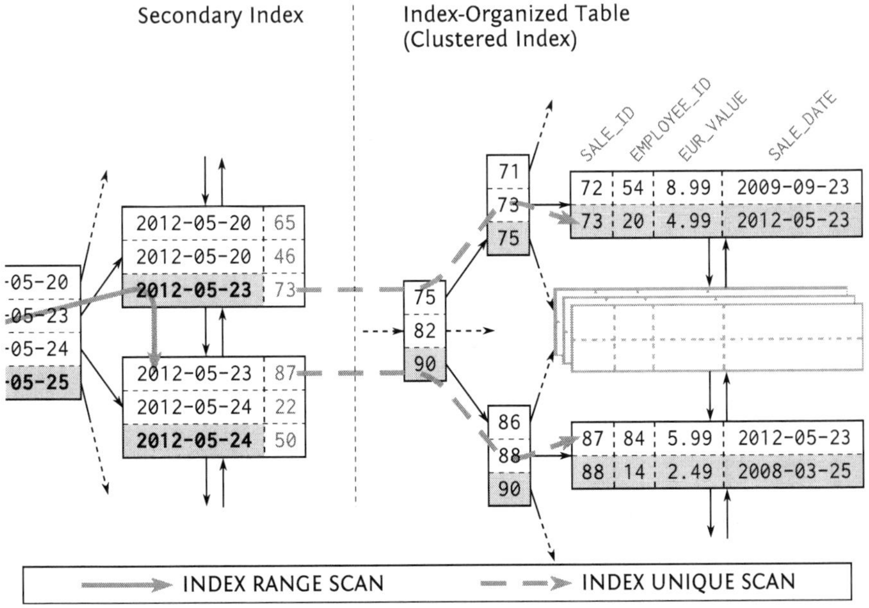

Figure 5.2 makes it clear, that the B-tree of the clustered index stands between the secondary index and the table data.

Accessing an index-organized table via a secondary index is very inefficient, and it can be prevented in the same way one prevents a table access on a heap table: by using an index-only scan—in this case better described as "secondary-index-only scan". The performance advantage of an index-only scan is even bigger because it not only prevents a single access but an entire INDEX UNIQUE SCAN.

> **IMPORTANT**
> Accessing an index-organized table via a secondary index is very inefficient.

124

INDEX-ORGANIZED TABLES

Using this example we can also see that databases exploit all the redundancies they have. Bear in mind that a secondary index stores the clustering key for each index entry. Consequently, we can query the clustering key from a secondary index without accessing the index-organized table:

```
SELECT sale_id
  FROM sales_iot
 WHERE sale_date = ?;


---------------------------------------------------
| Id | Operation         | Name           | Cost |
---------------------------------------------------
|  0 | SELECT STATEMENT  |                |   4  |
|* 1 |   INDEX RANGE SCAN| SALES_IOT_DATE |   4  |
---------------------------------------------------

Predicate Information (identified by operation id):
---------------------------------------------------
   1 - access("SALE_DATE"=:DT)
```

The table SALES_IOT is an index-organized table that uses SALE_ID as clustering key. Although the index SALE_IOT_DATE is on the SALE_DATE column only, it still has a copy of the clustering key SALE_ID so it can satisfy the query using the secondary index only.

When selecting other columns, the database has to run an INDEX UNIQUE SCAN on the clustered index for each row:

```
SELECT eur_value
  FROM sales_iot
 WHERE sale_date = ?;


----------------------------------------------------
| Id  | Operation         | Name           | Cost |
----------------------------------------------------
|   0 | SELECT STATEMENT  |                |  13  |
|*  1 |   INDEX UNIQUE SCAN| SALES_IOT_PK  |  13  |
|*  2 |    INDEX RANGE SCAN| SALES_IOT_DATE |   4  |
----------------------------------------------------

Predicate Information (identified by operation id):
----------------------------------------------------
   1 - access("SALE_DATE"=:DT)
   2 - access("SALE_DATE"=:DT)
```

Index-organized tables and clustered indexes are, after all, not as useful as it seems at first sight. Performance improvements on the clustered index are easily lost on when using a secondary index. The clustering key is usually longer than a ROWID so that the secondary indexes are larger than they would be on a heap table, often eliminating the savings from the omission of the heap table. The strength of index-organized tables and clustered indexes is mostly limited to tables that do not need a second index. Heap tables have the benefit of providing a stationary master copy that can be easily referenced.

> **IMPORTANT**
>
> Tables with one index only are best implemented as clustered indexes or index-organized tables.
>
> Tables with more indexes can often benefit from heap tables. You can still use index-only scans to avoid the table access. This gives you the `select` performance of a clustered index without slowing down other indexes.

Database support for index-organized tables and clustered index is very inconsistent. The overview on the next page explains the most important specifics.

WHY SECONDARY INDEXES HAVE NO ROWID

A direct pointer to the table row would be desirable for a secondary index as well. But that is only possible, if the table row stays at fixed storage positions. That is, unfortunately, not possible if the row is part of an index structure, which is kept in order. Keeping the index order needs to move rows occasionally. This is also true for operations that do not affect the row itself. An `insert` statement, for example, might split a leaf node to gain space for the new entry. That means that some entries are moved to a new data block at a different place.

A heap table, on the other hand, doesn't keep the rows in any order. The database saves new entries wherever it finds enough space. Once written, data doesn't move in heap tables.

Index-Organized Tables

MySQL

> The MyISAM engine only uses heap tables while the InnoDB engine always uses clustered indexes. That means you do not directly have a choice.

Oracle Database

> The Oracle database uses heap tables by default. Index-organized tables can be created using the ORGANIZATION INDEX clause:

```
CREATE TABLE (
    id    NUMBER NOT NULL PRIMARY KEY,
    [...]
) ORGANIZATION INDEX;
```

> The Oracle database always uses the primary key as the clustering key.

PostgreSQL

> PostgreSQL only uses heap tables.

> You can, however, use the CLUSTER clause to align the contents of the heap table with an index.

SQL Server

> By default SQL Server uses clustered indexes (index-organized tables) using the primary key as clustering key. Nevertheless you can use arbitrary columns for the clustering key—even non-unique columns.

> To create a heap table you must use the NONCLUSTERED clause in the primary key definition:

```
CREATE TABLE (
    id    NUMBER NOT NULL,
    [...]
    CONSTRAINT pk PRIMARY KEY NONCLUSTERED (id)
);
```

> Dropping a clustered index transforms the table into a heap table.

> SQL Server's default behavior often causes performance problems when using secondary indexes.

CHAPTER 6

SORTING AND GROUPING

Sorting is a very resource intensive operation. It needs a fair amount of CPU time, but the main problem is that the database must temporarily buffer the results. After all, a sort operation must read the complete input before it can produce the first output. Sort operations cannot be executed in a pipelined manner—this can become a problem for large data sets.

An index provides an ordered representation of the indexed data: this principle was already described in Chapter 1. We could also say that an index stores the data in a presorted fashion. The index is, in fact, sorted just like when using the index definition in an **order by** clause. It is therefore no surprise that we can use indexes to avoid the sort operation to satisfy an **order by** clause.

Ironically, an INDEX RANGE SCAN also becomes inefficient for large data sets—especially when followed by a table access. This can nullify the savings from avoiding the sort operation. A FULL TABLE SCAN with an explicit sort operation might be even faster in this case. Again, it is the optimizer's job to evaluate the different execution plans and select the best one.

An indexed **order by** execution not only saves the sorting effort, however; it is also able to return the first results without processing all input data. The **order by** is thus executed in a *pipelined* manner. Chapter 7, "Partial Results", explains how to exploit the pipelined execution to implement efficient pagination queries. This makes the pipelined **order by** so important that I refer to it as the *third power of indexing*.

This chapter explains how to use an index for a pipelined **order by** execution. To this end we have to pay special attention to the interactions with the **where** clause and also to ASC and DESC modifiers. The chapter concludes by applying these techniques to **group by** clauses as well.

129

CHAPTER 6: SORTING AND GROUPING

INDEXING ORDER BY

SQL queries with an order by clause do not need to sort the result explicitly if the relevant index already delivers the rows in the required order. That means the same index that is used for the where clause must also cover the order by clause.

As an example, consider the following query that selects yesterday's sales ordered by sale data and product ID:

```
SELECT sale_date, product_id, quantity
  FROM sales
 WHERE sale_date = TRUNC(sysdate) - INTERVAL '1' DAY
 ORDER BY sale_date, product_id;
```

There is already an index on SALE_DATE that can be used for the where clause. The database must, however, perform an explicit sort operation to satisfy the order by clause:

```
---------------------------------------------------------------
|Id | Operation                   | Name       | Rows | Cost |
---------------------------------------------------------------
| 0 | SELECT STATEMENT            |            | 320 |   18 |
| 1 |  SORT ORDER BY              |            | 320 |   18 |
| 2 |   TABLE ACCESS BY INDEX ROWID| SALES     | 320 |   17 |
|*3 |    INDEX RANGE SCAN         | SALES_DATE | 320 |    3 |
---------------------------------------------------------------
```

An INDEX RANGE SCAN delivers the result in index order anyway. To take advantage of this fact, we just have to extend the index definition so it corresponds to the order by clause:

```
  DROP INDEX sales_date;
CREATE INDEX sales_dt_pr ON sales (sale_date, product_id);
```

```
---------------------------------------------------------------
|Id | Operation                   | Name        | Rows | Cost |
---------------------------------------------------------------
| 0 | SELECT STATEMENT            |             | 320 |  300 |
| 1 |  TABLE ACCESS BY INDEX ROWID| SALES       | 320 |  300 |
|*2 |   INDEX RANGE SCAN          | SALES_DT_PR | 320 |    4 |
---------------------------------------------------------------
```

130

INDEXING ORDER BY

The sort operation SORT ORDER BY disappeared from the execution plan even though the query still has an **order by** clause. The database exploits the index order and skips the explicit sort operation.

> **IMPORTANT**
>
> If the index order corresponds to the **order by** clause, the database can omit the explicit sort operation.

Even though the new execution plan has fewer operations, the cost value has increased considerably because the clustering factor of the new index is worse (see "Automatically Optimized Clustering Factor" on page 133). At this point, it should just be noted that the cost value is not always a good indicator of the execution effort.

For this optimization, it is sufficient that the scanned index range is sorted according to the **order by** clause. Thus the optimization also works for this particular example when sorting by PRODUCT_ID only:

```
SELECT sale_date, product_id, quantity
  FROM sales
 WHERE sale_date = TRUNC(sysdate) - INTERVAL '1' DAY
 ORDER BY product_id;
```

In Figure 6.1 we can see that the PRODUCT_ID is the only relevant sort criterion in the scanned index range. Hence the index order corresponds to the **order by** clause in *this index range* so that the database can omit the sort operation.

Figure 6.1. Sort Order in the Relevant Index Range

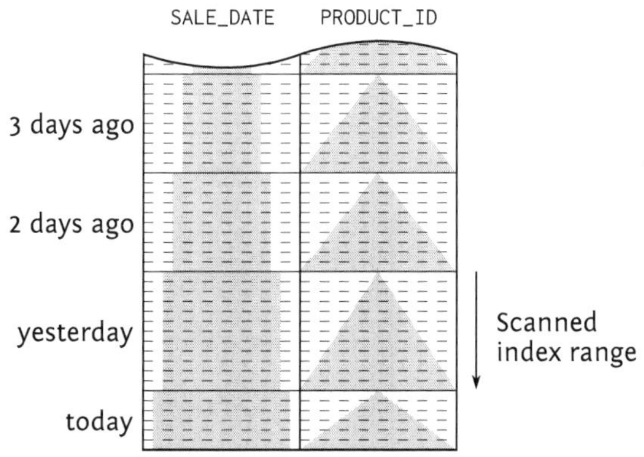

131

CHAPTER 6: SORTING AND GROUPING

This optimization can cause unexpected behavior when extending the scanned index range:

```
SELECT sale_date, product_id, quantity
  FROM sales
 WHERE sale_date >= TRUNC(sysdate) - INTERVAL '1' DAY
 ORDER BY product_id;
```

This query does not retrieve *yesterday's* sales but all sales *since yesterday*. That means it covers several days and scans an index range that is not exclusively sorted by the PRODUCT_ID. If we look at Figure 6.1 again and extend the scanned index range to the bottom, we can see that there are again smaller PRODUCT_ID values. The database must therefore use an explicit sort operation to satisfy the **order by** clause.

```
---------------------------------------------------------------
|Id |Operation                    | Name       | Rows | Cost |
---------------------------------------------------------------
| 0 |SELECT STATEMENT             |            | 320  | 301  |
| 1 | SORT ORDER BY               |            | 320  | 301  |
| 2 |  TABLE ACCESS BY INDEX ROWID| SALES      | 320  | 300  |
|*3 |   INDEX RANGE SCAN          | SALES_DT_PR| 320  |   4  |
---------------------------------------------------------------
```

If the database uses a sort operation even though you expected a pipelined execution, it can have two reasons: (1) the execution plan with the explicit sort operation has a better cost value; (2) the index order in the scanned index range does not correspond to the **order by** clause.

A simple way to tell the two cases apart is to use the full index definition in the **order by** clause—that means adjusting the query to the index in order to eliminate the second cause. If the database still uses an explicit sort operation, the optimizer prefers this plan due to its cost value; otherwise the database cannot use the index for the original **order by** clause.

> **TIP**
>
> Use the full index definition in the **order by** clause to find the reason for an explicit sort operation.

132

In both cases, you might wonder if and how you could possibly reach a pipelined **order by** execution. For this you can execute the query with the full index definition in the **order by** clause and inspect the result. You will often realize that you have a false perception of the index and that the index order is indeed not as required by the original **order by** clause so the database cannot use the index to avoid a sort operation.

If the optimizer prefers an explicit sort operation for its cost value, it is usually because the optimizer takes the best execution plan for the *full execution* of the query. In other words, the optimizer opts for the execution plan which is the fastest to get the last record. If the database detects that the application fetches only the first few rows, it might in turn prefer an indexed **order by**. Chapter 7, "Partial Results", explains the corresponding optimization methods.

AUTOMATICALLY OPTIMIZED CLUSTERING FACTOR

The Oracle database keeps the clustering factor at a minimum by considering the ROWID for the index order. Whenever two index entries have the same key values, the ROWID decides upon their final order. The index is therefore also ordered according to the table order and thus has the smallest possible clustering factor because the ROWID represents the physical address of table row.

By adding another column to an index, you insert a new sort criterion *before* the ROWID. The database has less freedom in aligning the index entries according to the table order so the index clustering factor can only get worse.

Regardless, it is still possible that the index order roughly corresponds to the table order. The sales of a day are probably still clustered together in the table as well as in the index—even though their sequence is not exactly the same anymore. The database has to read the table blocks multiple times when using the SALE_DT_PR index—but these are just the same table blocks as before. Due to the caching of frequently accessed data, the performance impact could be considerably lower than indicated by the cost values.

CHAPTER 6: SORTING AND GROUPING

INDEXING ASC, DESC AND NULLS FIRST/LAST

Databases can read indexes in both directions. That means that a pipelined order by is also possible if the scanned index range is in the exact opposite order as specified by the order by clause. Although ASC and DESC modifiers in the order by clause can prevent a pipelined execution, most databases offer a simple way to change the index order so an index becomes usable for a pipelined order by.

The following example uses an index in reverse order. It delivers the sales since yesterday ordered by descending date and descending PRODUCT_ID.

```
SELECT sale_date, product_id, quantity
  FROM sales
 WHERE sale_date >= TRUNC(sysdate) - INTERVAL '1' DAY
 ORDER BY sale_date DESC, product_id DESC;
```

The execution plan shows that the database reads the index in a descending direction.

```
-------------------------------------------------------------
|Id |Operation                     | Name       | Rows | Cost |
-------------------------------------------------------------
| 0 |SELECT STATEMENT              |            | 320 |  300 |
| 1 | TABLE ACCESS BY INDEX ROWID  | SALES      | 320 |  300 |
|*2 |  INDEX RANGE SCAN DESCENDING | SALES_DT_PR | 320 |   4 |
-------------------------------------------------------------
```

In this case, the database uses the index tree to find the *last* matching entry. From there on, it follows the leaf node chain "upwards" as shown in Figure 6.2. After all, this is why the database uses a *doubly* linked list to build the leaf node chain.

Of course it is crucial that the scanned index range is in the exact opposite order as needed for the order by clause.

IMPORTANT

Databases can read indexes in both directions.

134

INDEXING ASC, DESC AND NULLS FIRST/LAST

Figure 6.2. Reverse Index Scan

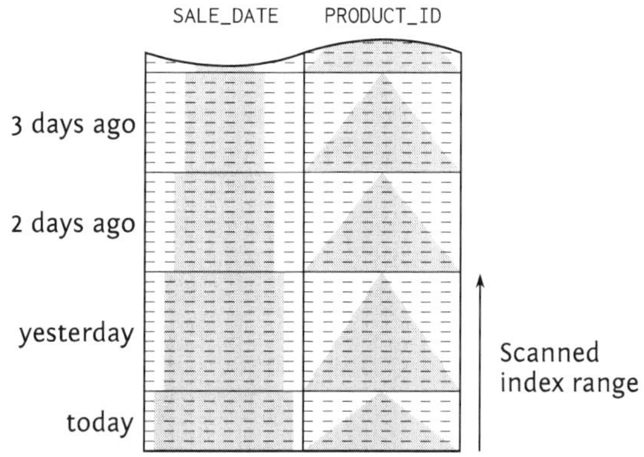

The following example does not fulfill this prerequisite because it mixes ASC and DESC modifiers in the **order by** clause:

```
SELECT sale_date, product_id, quantity
  FROM sales
 WHERE sale_date >= TRUNC(sysdate) - INTERVAL '1' DAY
 ORDER BY sale_date ASC, product_id DESC;
```

The query must first deliver yesterday's sales ordered by descending PRODUCT_ID and then today's sales, again by descending PRODUCT_ID. Figure 6.3 illustrates this process. To get the sales in the required order, the database would have to "jump" during the index scan.

Figure 6.3. Impossible Pipelined **order by**

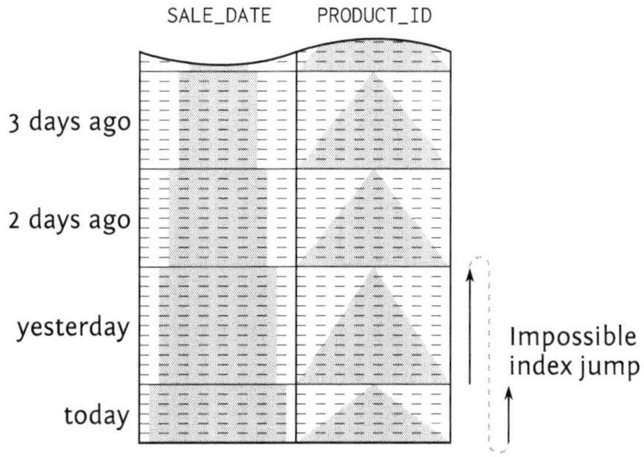

CHAPTER 6: SORTING AND GROUPING

However, the index has no link from yesterday's sale with the smallest PRODUCT_ID to today's sale with the greatest. The database can therefore not use this index to avoid an explicit sort operation.

For cases like this, most databases offer a simple method to adjust the index order to the **order by** clause. Concretely, this means that you can use ASC and DESC modifiers in the index declaration:

```
DROP INDEX sales_dt_pr;

CREATE INDEX sales_dt_pr
    ON sales (sale_date ASC, product_id DESC);
```

> **WARNING**
>
> Prior to version 8.0, the MySQL database ignores ASC and DESC modifiers in the index definition.

Now the index order corresponds to the **order by** clause so the database can omit the sort operation:

```
---------------------------------------------------------------
|Id | Operation                  | Name        | Rows | Cost |
---------------------------------------------------------------
| 0 | SELECT STATEMENT           |             | 320  | 301  |
| 1 |  TABLE ACCESS BY INDEX ROWID| SALES      | 320  | 301  |
|*2 |   INDEX RANGE SCAN         | SALES_DT_PR | 320  |   4  |
---------------------------------------------------------------
```

Figure 6.4 shows the new index order. The change in the sort direction for the second column in a way swaps the direction of the arrows from the previous figure. That makes the first arrow end where the second arrow starts so that index has the rows in the desired order.

> **IMPORTANT**
>
> When using mixed ASC and DESC modifiers in the **order by** clause, you must define the index likewise in order to use it for a pipelined **order by**.
>
> This does not affect the index's usability for the **where** clause.

136

INDEXING ASC, DESC AND NULLS FIRST/LAST

Figure 6.4. Mixed-Order Index

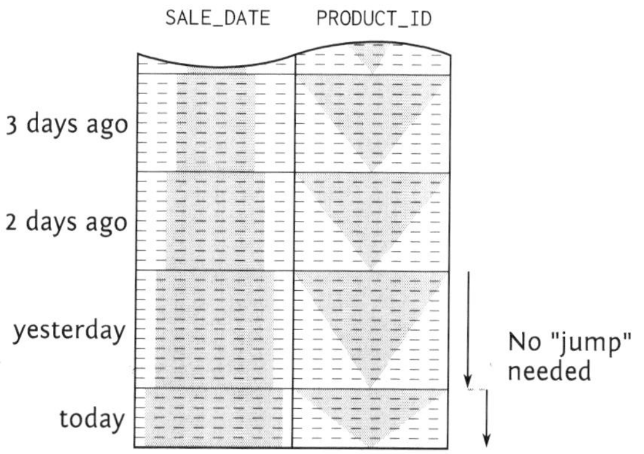

ASC/DESC indexing is only needed for sorting individual columns in opposite direction. It is not needed to reverse the order of all columns because the database could still read the index in descending order if needed—secondary indexes on index organized tables being the only exception. Secondary indexes implicitly add the clustering key to the index without providing any possibility for specifying the sort order. If you need to sort the clustering key in descending order, you have no other option than sorting all other columns in descending order. The database can then read the index in reverse direction to get the desired order.

Besides ASC and DESC, the SQL standard defines two hardly known modifiers for the **order by** clause: NULLS FIRST and NULLS LAST. Explicit control over NULL sorting was "recently" introduced as an *optional* extension with SQL:2003. As a consequence, database support is sparse. This is particularly worrying because the standard does not exactly define the sort order of NULL. It only states that all NULLs must appear together after sorting, but it does not specify if they should appear before or after the other entries. Strictly speaking, you would actually need to specify NULL sorting for all columns that can be null in the **order by** clause to get a well-defined behavior.

The fact is, however, that the optional extension is neither implemented by SQL Server 2017 nor by MySQL 8.0. The Oracle database, on the contrary, supported NULLS sorting even before it was introduced to the standard, but it does not accept it in index definitions as of release 12c. The Oracle database can therefore not do a pipelined **order by** when sorting with

CHAPTER 6: SORTING AND GROUPING

NULLS FIRST. Only the PostgreSQL database (since release 8.3) supports the NULLS modifier in both the **order by** clause and the index definition.

The following overview summarizes the features provided by different databases.

Figure 6.5. Database/Feature Matrix

	DB2	MySQL	Oracle	PostgreSQL	SQLite	SQL Server
Read index backwards	✔	✔	✔	✔	✔	✔
Order by ASC/DESC	✔	✔	✔	✔	✔	✔
Index ASC/DESC	✔	✗	✔	✔	✔	✔
Order by NULLS FIRST/LAST	✗	✗	✔	✔	✗	✗
Default NULLS order	First	First	Last	Last	First	First
Index NULLS FIRST/LAST	✗	✗	✗	✔	✗	✗

Indexing Group By

SQL databases use two entirely different **group by** algorithms. The first one, the hash algorithm, aggregates the input records in a temporary hash table. Once all input records are processed, the hash table is returned as the result. The second algorithm, the sort/group algorithm, first sorts the input data by the grouping key so that the rows of each group follow each other in immediate succession. Afterwards, the database just needs to aggregate them. In general, both algorithms need to materialize an intermediate state, so they are not executed in a pipelined manner. Nevertheless the sort/group algorithm can use an index to avoid the sort operation, thus enabling a pipelined **group by**.

> **NOTE**
>
> MySQL 5.7 doesn't use the hash algorithm. Nevertheless, the optimization for the sort/group algorithm works as described below.

Consider the following query. It delivers yesterday's revenue grouped by PRODUCT_ID:

```
SELECT product_id, sum(eur_value)
  FROM sales
 WHERE sale_date = TRUNC(sysdate) - INTERVAL '1' DAY
 GROUP BY product_id;
```

Knowing the index on SALE_DATE and PRODUCT_ID from the previous section, the sort/group algorithm is more appropriate because an INDEX RANGE SCAN automatically delivers the rows in the required order. That means the database avoids materialization because it does not need an explicit sort operation—the **group by** is executed in a pipelined manner.

```
---------------------------------------------------------------
|Id |Operation                    | Name        | Rows | Cost |
---------------------------------------------------------------
| 0 |SELECT STATEMENT             |             |   17 |  192 |
| 1 | SORT GROUP BY NOSORT        |             |   17 |  192 |
| 2 |  TABLE ACCESS BY INDEX ROWID| SALES       |  321 |  192 |
|*3 |   INDEX RANGE SCAN          | SALES_DT_PR |  321 |    3 |
---------------------------------------------------------------
```

139

CHAPTER 6: SORTING AND GROUPING

The Oracle database's execution plan marks a pipelined SORT GROUP BY operation with the NOSORT addendum. The execution plan of other databases does not mention any sort operation at all.

The pipelined **group by** has the same prerequisites as the pipelined **order by**, except there are no ASC and DESC modifiers. That means that defining an index with ASC/DESC modifiers should not affect pipelined **group by** execution. The same is true for NULLS FIRST/LAST. Nevertheless there are databases that cannot properly use an ASC/DESC index for a pipelined **group by**.

WARNING

For PostgreSQL, you must add an **order by** clause to make an index with NULLS LAST sorting usable for a pipelined **group by**.

The Oracle database cannot read an index backwards in order to execute a pipelined **group by** that is followed by an **order by**.

If we extend the query to consider all sales *since yesterday*, as we did in the example for the pipelined **order by**, it prevents the pipelined **group by** for the same reason as before: the INDEX RANGE SCAN does not deliver the rows ordered by the grouping key (compare Figure 6.1 on page 131).

```
SELECT product_id, sum(eur_value)
  FROM sales
 WHERE sale_date >= TRUNC(sysdate) - INTERVAL '1' DAY
 GROUP BY product_id;
```

```
-----------------------------------------------------------------
|Id |Operation                     | Name        | Rows | Cost |
-----------------------------------------------------------------
| 0 |SELECT STATEMENT              |             |   24 |  356 |
| 1 | HASH GROUP BY                |             |   24 |  356 |
| 2 |  TABLE ACCESS BY INDEX ROWID | SALES       |  596 |  355 |
|*3 |   INDEX RANGE SCAN           | SALES_DT_PR |  596 |    4 |
-----------------------------------------------------------------
```

Instead, the Oracle database uses the hash algorithm. The advantage of the hash algorithm is that it only needs to buffer the *aggregated result*, whereas the sort/group algorithm materializes the *complete input set*. In other words: the hash algorithm needs less memory.

140

INDEXING GROUP BY

As with pipelined **order by**, a fast execution is not the most important aspect of the pipelined **group by** execution. It is more important that the database executes it in a pipelined manner and delivers the first result before reading the entire input. This is the prerequisite for the advanced optimization methods explained in the next chapter.

> ### THINK ABOUT IT
> Can you think of any other database operation—besides sorting and grouping—that could possibly use an index to avoid sorting?

CHAPTER 7

PARTIAL RESULTS

Sometimes you do not need the full result of an SQL query but only the first few rows — e.g., to show only the ten most recent messages. In this case, it is also common to allow users to browse through older messages — either using traditional paging navigation or the more modern "infinite scrolling" variant. The related SQL queries used for this function can, however, cause serious performance problems if *all* messages must be sorted in order to find the most recent ones. A pipelined **order by** is therefore a very powerful means of optimization for such queries.

This chapter demonstrates how to use a pipelined **order by** to efficiently retrieve partial results. Although the syntax of these queries varies from database to database, they still execute the queries in a very similar way. Once again, this illustrates that they all put their pants on one leg at a time.

QUERYING TOP-N ROWS

Top-N queries are queries that limit the result to a specific number of rows. These are often queries for the most recent or the "best" entries of a result set. For efficient execution, the ranking must be done with a pipelined **order by**.

The simplest way to fetch only the first rows of a query is fetching the required rows and then closing the statement. Unfortunately, the optimizer cannot foresee that when preparing the execution plan. To select the best execution plan, the optimizer has to know if the application will ultimately fetch all rows. In that case, a full table scan with explicit sort operation might perform best, although a pipelined **order by** could be better when fetching only ten rows — even if the database has to fetch each row individually. That means that the optimizer has to know if you are going to abort the statement before fetching all rows so it can select the best execution plan.

143

CHAPTER 7: PARTIAL RESULTS

> 💡 **TIP**
>
> Inform the database whenever you don't need all rows.

The SQL standard excluded this requirement for a long time. The corresponding extension (**fetch first**) was finally introduced with SQL:2008 and is currently available in IBM DB2, PostgreSQL, SQL Server 2012 and Oracle 12c. On the one hand, this is because the feature is a non-core extension, and on the other hand it's because each database has been offering its own proprietary solution for many years.

The following examples show the use of these well-known extensions by querying the ten most recent sales. The basis is always the same: fetching *all* sales, beginning with the most recent one. The respective top-N syntax just aborts the execution after fetching ten rows.

MYSQL

MySQL and PostgreSQL use the `limit` clause to restrict the number of rows to be fetched.

```
SELECT *
  FROM sales
 ORDER BY sale_date DESC
 LIMIT 10;
```

ORACLE DATABASE

The Oracle database introduced the **fetch first** extension with release 12c. With earlier releases you have to use the pseudo column ROWNUM that numbers the rows in the result set automatically. To use this column in a filter, we have to wrap the query:

```
SELECT *
  FROM (
        SELECT *
          FROM sales
         ORDER BY sale_date DESC
       )
 WHERE rownum <= 10;
```

144

QUERYING TOP-N ROWS

POSTGRESQL

PostgreSQL supports the **fetch first** extension since version 8.4. The previously used **limit** clause still works as shown in the MySQL example.

```
SELECT *
  FROM sales
  ORDER BY sale_date DESC
  FETCH FIRST 10 ROWS ONLY;
```

SQL SERVER

SQL Server provides the **top** clause to restrict the number of rows to be fetched.

```
SELECT TOP 10 *
  FROM sales
  ORDER BY sale_date DESC;
```

Starting with release 2012, SQL Server supports the **fetch first** extension as well.

All of the above shown SQL queries are special because the databases recognize them as top-N queries.

IMPORTANT

The database can only optimize a query for a partial result if it knows this from the beginning.

If the optimizer is aware of the fact that we only need ten rows, it will prefer to use a pipelined **order by** if applicable:

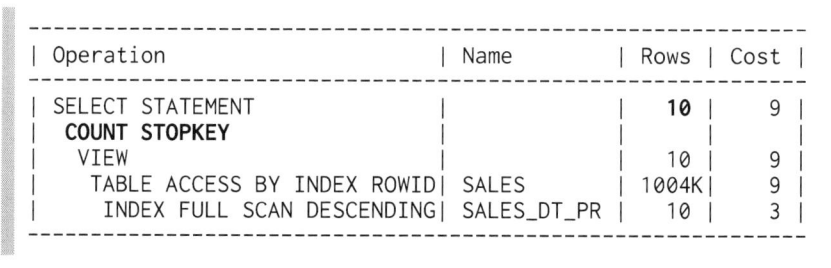

```
---------------------------------------------------------------
| Operation                     | Name       | Rows  | Cost |
---------------------------------------------------------------
| SELECT STATEMENT              |            | 10    |   9  |
| COUNT STOPKEY                 |            |       |      |
|  VIEW                         |            | 10    |   9  |
|   TABLE ACCESS BY INDEX ROWID | SALES      | 1004K |   9  |
|    INDEX FULL SCAN DESCENDING | SALES_DT_PR| 10    |   3  |
---------------------------------------------------------------
```

The Oracle execution plan indicates the planned termination with the COUNT STOPKEY operation. That means the database recognized the top-N syntax.

145

CHAPTER 7: PARTIAL RESULTS

> **TIP**
>
> Appendix A, *"Execution Plans"*, summarizes the corresponding operations for MySQL, Oracle, PostgreSQL and SQL Server.

Using the correct syntax is only half the story because efficiently terminating the execution requires the underlying operations to be executed in a pipelined manner. That means the **order by** clause must be covered by an index—the index SALE_DT_PR on SALE_DATE and PRODUCT_ID in this example. By using this index, the database can avoid an explicit sort operation and so can immediately send the rows to the application as read from the index. The execution is aborted after fetching ten rows so the database does not read more rows than selected.

> **IMPORTANT**
>
> A pipelined top-N query doesn't need to read and sort the entire result set.

If there is no suitable index on SALE_DATE for a pipelined **order by**, the database must read and sort the entire table. The first row is only delivered after reading the last row from the table.

```
---------------------------------------------------------
| Operation             | Name  | Rows  |  Cost  |
---------------------------------------------------------
| SELECT STATEMENT      |       |    10 | 59558  |
|  COUNT STOPKEY        |       |       |        |
|   VIEW                |       | 1004K | 59558  |
|    SORT ORDER BY STOPKEY|     | 1004K | 59558  |
|     TABLE ACCESS FULL | SALES | 1004K |  9246  |
---------------------------------------------------------
```

This execution plan has no pipelined **order by** and is almost as slow as aborting the execution from the client side. Using the top-N syntax is still better because the database does not need to materialize the full result but only the ten most recent rows. This requires considerably less memory. The Oracle execution plan indicates this optimization with the STOPKEY modifier on the SORT ORDER BY operation.

The advantages of a pipelined top-N query include not only immediate performance gains but also improved scalability. Without using pipelined execution, the response time of this top-N query grows with the table size. The response time using a pipelined execution, however, only grows

146

with the number of selected rows. In other words, the response time of a pipelined top-N query is always the same; this is almost independent of the table size. Only when the B-tree depth grows does the query become a little bit slower.

Figure 7.1 shows the scalability for both variants over a growing volume of data. The linear response time growth for an execution without a pipelined **order by** is clearly visible. The response time for the pipelined execution remains constant.

Figure 7.1. Scalability of Top-N Queries

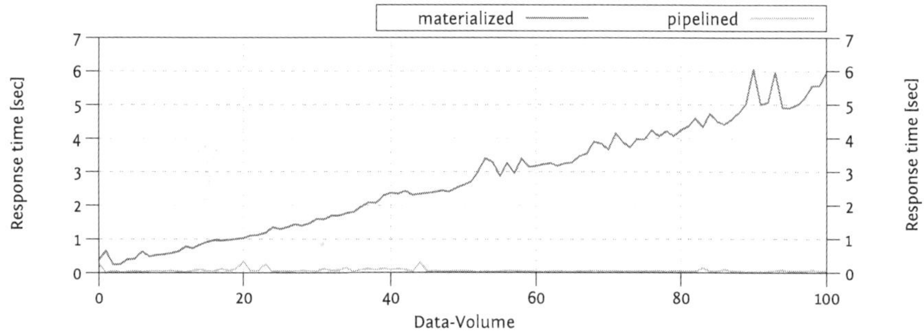

Although the response time of a pipelined top-N query does not depend on the table size, it still grows with the number of selected rows. The response time will therefore double when selecting twice as many rows. This is particularly significant for "paging" queries that load additional results because these queries often start at the first entry again; they will read the rows already shown on the previous page and discard them before finally reaching the results for the second page. Nevertheless, there is a solution for this problem as well as we will see in the next section.

PAGING THROUGH RESULTS

After implementing a pipelined top-N query to retrieve the first page efficiently, you will often also need another query to fetch the next pages. The resulting challenge is that it has to skip the rows from the previous pages. There are two different methods to meet this challenge: firstly the *offset method*, which numbers the rows from the beginning and uses a filter on this row number to discard the rows before the requested page. The second method, which I call the *seek method*, searches the last entry of the previous page and fetches only the following rows.

CHAPTER 7: PARTIAL RESULTS

The following examples show the more widely used offset method. Its main advantage is that it is very easy to handle—especially with databases that have a dedicated keyword for it (offset). This keyword was even taken into the SQL standard as part of the fetch first extension.

MYSQL

MySQL and PostgreSQL offer the offset clause for discarding the specified number of rows from the beginning of a top-N query. The limit clause is applied afterwards.

```
SELECT *
  FROM sales
 ORDER BY sale_date DESC
 LIMIT 10 OFFSET 10;
```

ORACLE DATABASE

The Oracle database supports offset since release 12c. Alternativley, the pseudo column ROWNUM can be used to number the rows. It is, however, not possible to apply a greater than or equal to (>=) filter on this pseudo-column. To make this work, you need to first "materialize" the row numbers by renaming the column with an alias.

```
SELECT *
  FROM ( SELECT tmp.*, rownum rn
           FROM ( SELECT *
                    FROM sales
                   ORDER BY sale_date DESC
                ) tmp
          WHERE rownum <= 20
       )
 WHERE rn > 10;
```

Note the use of the alias RN for the lower bound and the ROWNUM pseudo column itself for the upper bound.

POSTGRESQL

The fetch first extension defines an offset ... rows clause as well. PostgreSQL, however, only accepts offset without the rows keyword. The previously used limit/offset syntax still works as shown in the MySQL example.

```
SELECT *
  FROM sales
 ORDER BY sale_date DESC
 OFFSET 10
 FETCH NEXT 10 ROWS ONLY;
```

148

SQL Server

SQL Server does not have an "offset" extension for its proprietary **top** clause but introduced the **fetch first** extension with SQL Server 2012. The **offset** clause is mandatory although the standard defines it as an optional addendum.

```
SELECT *
  FROM sales
  ORDER BY sale_date DESC
 OFFSET 10 ROWS
 FETCH NEXT 10 ROWS ONLY;
```

Besides the simplicity, another advantage of this method is that you just need the row offset to fetch an arbitrary page. Nevertheless, the database must count all rows from the beginning until it reaches the requested page. Figure 7.2 shows that the scanned index range becomes greater when fetching more pages.

Figure 7.2. Access Using the Offset Method

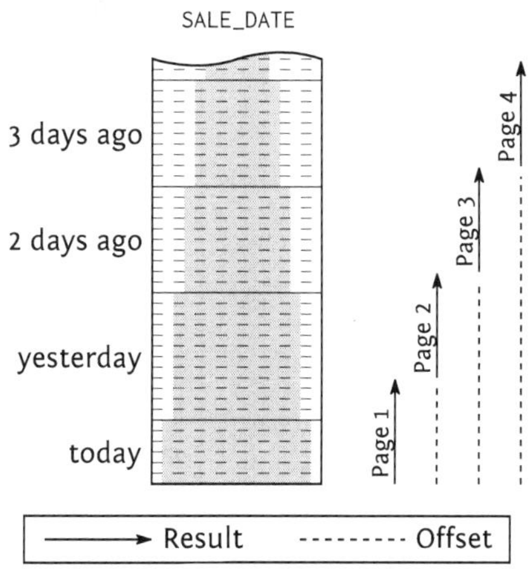

This has two disadvantages: (1) the pages drift when inserting new sales because the numbering is always done from scratch; (2) the response time increases when browsing further back.

The seek method avoids both problems because it uses the *values* of the previous page as a delimiter. That means it searches for the values that must *come behind* the last entry from the previous page. This can be expressed with a simple **where** clause. To put it the other way around: the seek method simply doesn't select already shown values.

CHAPTER 7: PARTIAL RESULTS

The next example shows the seek method. For the sake of demonstration, we will start with the assumption that there is only one sale per day. This makes the SALE_DATE a unique key. To select the sales that must come behind a particular date you must use a less than condition (<) because of the descending sort order. For an ascending order, you would have to use a greater than (>) condition. The **fetch first** clause is just used to limit the result to ten rows.

```
SELECT *
  FROM sales
 WHERE sale_date < ?
 ORDER BY sale_date DESC
 FETCH FIRST 10 ROWS ONLY;
```

Instead of a row number, you use the last value of the previous page to specify the lower bound. This has a huge benefit in terms of performance because the database can use the SALE_DATE < ? condition for index access. That means that the database can truly skip the rows from the previous pages. On top of that, you will also get stable results if new rows are inserted.

Nevertheless, this method does not work if there is more than one sale per day—as shown in Figure 7.2—because using the last date from the first page ("yesterday") skips *all* results from yesterday—not just the ones already shown on the first page. The problem is that the **order by** clause does not establish a deterministic row sequence. That is, however, prerequisite to using a simple range condition for the page breaks.

Without a deterministic **order by** clause, the database by definition does not deliver a deterministic row sequence. The only reason you *usually* get a consistent row sequence is that the database *usually* executes the query in the same way. Nevertheless, the database could in fact shuffle the rows having the same SALE_DATE and still fulfill the **order by** clause. In recent releases it might indeed happen that you get the result in a different order every time you run the query, not because the database shuffles the result intentionally but because the database might utilize parallel query execution. That means that the same execution plan can result in a different row sequence because the executing threads finish in a non-deterministic order.

IMPORTANT

Paging requires a deterministic sort order.

150

Even if the functional specifications only require sorting "by date, latest first", we as the developers must make sure the order by clause yields a deterministic row sequence. For this purpose, we might need to extend the order by clause with arbitrary columns just to make sure we get a deterministic row sequence. If the index that is used for the pipelined order by has additional columns, it is a good start to add them to the order by clause so we can continue using this index for the pipelined order by. If this still does not yield a deterministic sort order, just add any unique column(s) and extend the index accordingly.

In the following example, we extend the order by clause and the index with the primary key SALE_ID to get a deterministic row sequence. Furthermore, we must apply the "comes after" logic to both columns *together* to get the desired result:

```
CREATE INDEX sl_dtid ON sales (sale_date, sale_id);

SELECT *
  FROM sales
 WHERE (sale_date, sale_id) < (?, ?)
 ORDER BY sale_date DESC, sale_id DESC
 FETCH FIRST 10 ROWS ONLY;
```

The where clause uses the little-known "row values" syntax (see the box entitled "SQL Row Values"). It combines multiple values into a logical unit that is applicable to the regular comparison operators. As with scalar values, the less-than condition corresponds to "comes after" when sorting in descending order. That means the query considers only the sales that come after the given SALE_DATE, SALE_ID pair.

Even though the row values syntax is part of the SQL standard, only a few databases support it. SQL Server 2017 does not support row values at all. The Oracle database supports row values in principle, but cannot apply range operators on them (ORA-01796). MySQL evaluates row value expressions correctly but cannot use them as access predicate during an index access. PostgreSQL, however, supports the row value syntax *and* uses them to access the index if there is a corresponding index available.

CHAPTER 7: PARTIAL RESULTS

Nevertheless it is possible to use an approximated variant of the seek method with databases that do not properly support the row values—even though the approximation is not as elegant and efficient as row values in PostgreSQL. For this approximation, we must use "regular" comparisons to express the required logic as shown in this Oracle example:

```
SELECT *
  FROM ( SELECT *
           FROM sales
          WHERE sale_date <= ?
            AND NOT (sale_date = ? AND sale_id >= ?)
          ORDER BY sale_date DESC, sale_id DESC
       )
 WHERE rownum <= 10;
```

The **where** clause consists of two parts. The first part considers the SALE_DATE only and uses a less than or equal to (<=) condition—it selects more rows as needed. This part of the **where** clause is simple enough so that all databases can use it to access the index. The second part of the **where** clause removes the excess rows that were already shown on the previous page. The box entitled "Indexing Equivalent Logic" explains why the **where** clause is expressed this way.

The execution plan shows that the database uses the first part of the **where** clause as access predicate.

```
---------------------------------------------------------------------
|Id | Operation                      | Name    | Rows  | Cost |
---------------------------------------------------------------------
| 0 | SELECT STATEMENT               |         |    10 |    4 |
|*1 |   COUNT STOPKEY                |         |       |      |
| 2 |    VIEW                        |         |    10 |    4 |
| 3 |     TABLE ACCESS BY INDEX ROWID| SALES   | 50218 |    4 |
|*4 |      INDEX RANGE SCAN DESCENDING| SL_DTIT |     2 |    3 |
---------------------------------------------------------------------

Predicate Information (identified by operation id):
---------------------------------------------------
   1 - filter(ROWNUM<=10)
   4 - access("SALE_DATE"<=:SALE_DATE)
       filter("SALE_DATE"<>:SALE_DATE
           OR "SALE_ID"<TO_NUMBER(:SALE_ID))
```

The access predicates on SALE_DATE enables the database to skip over the days that were fully shown on previous pages. The second part of the **where** clause is a filter predicate only. That means that the database inspects a

152

few entries from the previous page again, but drops them immediately. Figure 7.3 shows the respective access path.

Figure 7.3. Access Using the Seek Method

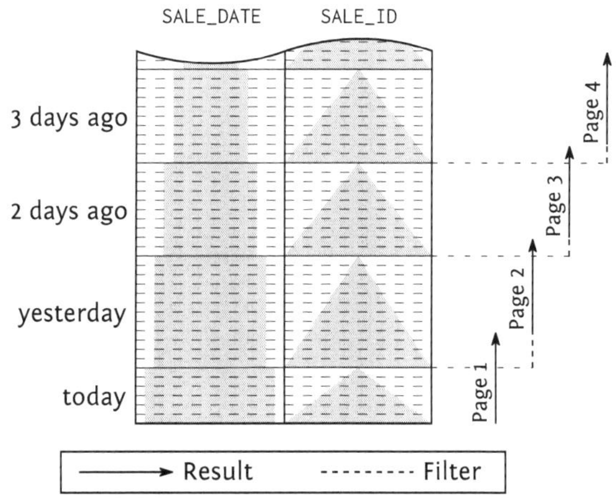

SQL ROW VALUES

Besides regular scalar values, the SQL standard also defines the so-called *row value constructors*. They "Specify an ordered set of values to be constructed into a row or partial row" [SQL:92, §7.1: <row value constructor>]. Syntactically, row values are lists in brackets. This syntax is best known for its use in the **insert** statement.

Using row value constructors in the **where** clause is, however, less well-known but still perfectly valid. The SQL standard actually defines all comparison operators for row value constructors. The definition for the less than operations is, for example, as follows:

"Rx < Ry" is true if and only if RXi = RYi for all i < n and RXn < RYn for some n.

—SQL:92, §8.2.7.2

Where *i* and *n* reflect positional indexes in the lists. That means a row value RX is less than RY if any value RXn is smaller than the corresponding RYn and all preceding value pairs are equal (*RXi = RYi; for i<n*).

This definition makes the expression RX < RY synonymous to "RX sorts before RY" which is exactly the logic we need for the seek method.

153

Figure 7.4 compares the performance characteristics of the offset and the seek methods. The accuracy of measurement is insufficient to see the difference on the left hand side of the chart, however the difference is clearly visible from about page 20 onwards.

Figure 7.4. Scalability when Fetching the Next Page

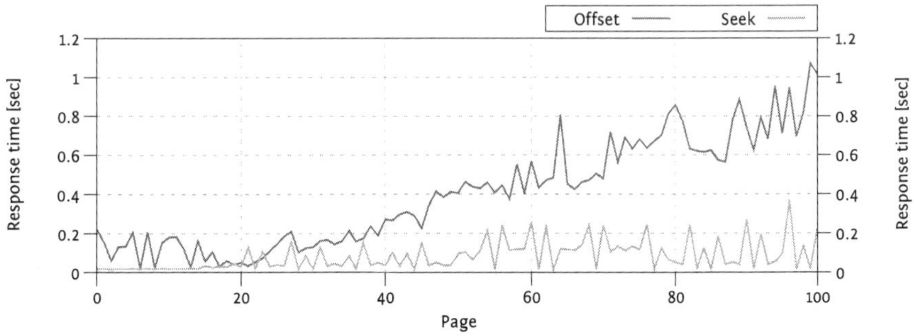

Of course the seek method has drawbacks as well, the difficulty in handling it being the most important one. You not only have to phrase the **where** clause very carefully—you also cannot fetch arbitrary pages. Moreover you need to reverse all comparison and sort operations to change the browsing direction. Precisely these two functions—skipping pages and browsing backwards—are not needed when using an infinite scrolling mechanism for the user interface.

INDEXING EQUIVALENT LOGIC

A logical condition can always be expressed in different ways. You could, for example, also implement the above shown skip logic as follows:

```
WHERE (
          (sale_date < ?)
      OR
          (sale_date = ? AND sale_id < ?)
      )
```

This variant only uses including conditions and is probably easier to understand—for human beings, at least. Databases have a different point of view. They do not recognize that the **where** clause selects all rows starting with the respective SALE_DATE/SALE_ID pair—provided that the SALE_DATE is the same for both branches. Instead, the database uses the entire **where** clause as filter predicate. We could at least expect the optimizer to "factor the condition SALE_DATE <= ? out" of the two or-branches, but none of the databases provides this service.

Nevertheless we can add this redundant condition manually—even though it does not increase readability:

```
WHERE sale_date <= ?
  AND (
          (sale_date < ?)
      OR
          (sale_date = ? AND sale_id < ?)
      )
```

Luckily, all databases are able to use the this part of the **where** clause as access predicate. That clause is, however, even harder to grasp as the approximation logic shown above. Further, the original logic avoids the risk that the "unnecessary" (redundant) part is accidentally removed from the **where** clause later on.

CHAPTER 7: PARTIAL RESULTS

Using Window Functions for Pagination

Window functions offer yet another way to implement pagination in SQL. This is a flexible, and above all, standards-compliant method. However, only SQL Server and the Oracle database can use them for a pipelined top-N query. MySQL[1] and PostgreSQL do not abort the index scan after fetching enough rows and therefore execute these queries very inefficiently.

The following example uses the window function ROW_NUMBER for a pagination query:

```
SELECT *
  FROM ( SELECT sales.*
              , ROW_NUMBER() OVER (ORDER BY sale_date DESC
                                         , sale_id   DESC) rn
           FROM sales
       ) tmp
 WHERE rn between 11 and 20
 ORDER BY sale_date DESC, sale_id DESC;
```

The ROW_NUMBER function enumerates the rows according to the sort order defined in the **over** clause. The outer **where** clause uses this enumeration to limit the result to the second page (rows 11 through 20).

The Oracle database recognizes the abort condition and uses the index on SALE_DATE and SALE_ID to produce a pipelined top-N behavior:

```
------------------------------------------------------------
|Id | Operation                    | Name    | Rows  | Cost  |
------------------------------------------------------------
| 0 | SELECT STATEMENT             |         | 1004K| 36877 |
|*1 |   VIEW                       |         | 1004K| 36877 |
|*2 |    WINDOW NOSORT STOPKEY      |         | 1004K| 36877 |
| 3 |     TABLE ACCESS BY INDEX ROWID | SALES | 1004K| 36877 |
| 4 |      INDEX FULL SCAN DESCENDING | SL_DTID | 1004K|  2955 |
------------------------------------------------------------

Predicate Information (identified by operation id):
------------------------------------------------------
1 - filter("RN">=11 AND "RN"<=20)
2 - filter(ROW_NUMBER() OVER (
          ORDER BY "SALE_DATE" DESC, "SALE_ID" DESC )<=20)
```

MySQL supports window functions since version 8.0.

156

The WINDOW NOSORT STOPKEY operation indicates that there is no sort operation (NOSORT) and that the database aborts the execution when reaching the upper threshold (STOPKEY). Considering that the aborted operations are executed in a pipelined manner, it means that this query is as efficient as the offset method explained in the previous section.

The strength of window functions is not pagination, however, but analytical calculations. If you have never used window functions before, you should definitely spend a few hours studying the respective documentation.

CHAPTER 8

MODIFYING DATA

So far we have only discussed query performance, but SQL is not only about queries. It supports data manipulation as well. The respective commands—insert, delete, and update—form the so-called "data manipulation language" (DML)—a section of the SQL standard. The performance of these commands is for the most part negatively influenced by indexes.

An index is pure redundancy. It contains only data that is also stored in the table. During write operations, the database must keep those redundancies consistent. Specifically, it means that insert, delete and update not only affect the table but also the indexes that hold a copy of the affected data.

INSERT

The number of indexes on a table is the most dominant factor for insert performance. The more indexes a table has, the slower the execution becomes. The insert statement is the only operation that cannot directly benefit from indexing because it has no where clause.

Adding a new row to a table involves several steps. First, the database must find a place to store the row. For a regular heap table—which has no particular row order—the database can take any table block that has enough free space. This is a very simple and quick process, mostly executed in main memory. All the database has to do afterwards is to add the new entry to the respective data block.

159

CHAPTER 8: MODIFYING DATA

If there are indexes on the table, the database must make sure the new entry is also found via these indexes. For this reason it has to add the new entry to each and every index on that table. The number of indexes is therefore a multiplier for the cost of an insert statement.

Moreover, adding an entry to an index is much more expensive than inserting one into a heap structure because the database has to keep the index order and tree balance. That means the new entry cannot be written to any block—it belongs to a specific leaf node. Although the database uses the index tree itself to find the correct leaf node, it still has to read a few index blocks for the tree traversal.

Once the correct leaf node has been identified, the database confirms that there is enough free space left in this node. If not, the database splits the leaf node and distributes the entries between the old and a new node. This process also affects the reference in the corresponding branch node as that must be duplicated as well. Needless to say, the branch node can run out of space as well so it might have to be split too. In the worst case, the database has to split all nodes up to the root node. This is the only case in which the tree gains an additional layer and grows in depth.

The index maintenance is, after all, the most expensive part of the insert operation. That is also visible in Figure 8.1, "Insert Performance by Number of Indexes": the execution time is hardly visible if the table does not have any indexes. Nevertheless, adding a single index is enough to increase the execute time by a factor of a hundred. Each additional index slows the execution down further.

Figure 8.1. Insert Performance by Number of Indexes

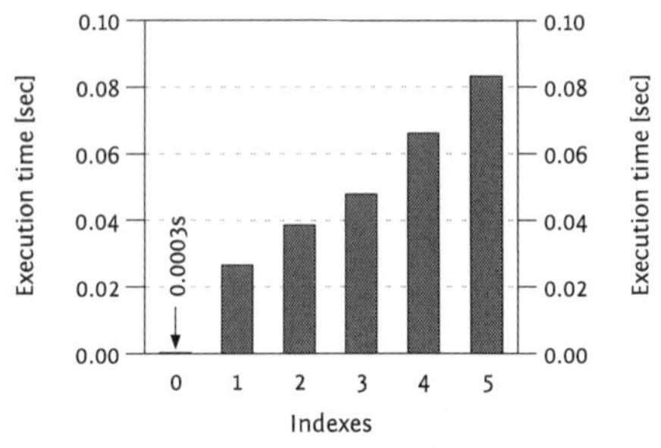

INSERT

> **NOTE**
> The first index makes the greatest difference.

To optimize `insert` performance, it is very important to keep the number of indexes small.

> **TIP**
> Use indexes deliberately and sparingly, and avoid redundant indexes whenever possible. This is also beneficial for `delete` and `update` statements.

Considering `insert` statements only, it would be best to avoid indexes entirely—this yields by far the best `insert` performance. However tables without indexes are rather unrealistic in real world applications. You usually want to retrieve the stored data again so that you need indexes to improve query speed. Even write-only log tables often have a primary key and a respective index.

Nevertheless, the performance without indexes is so good that it can make sense to temporarily drop all indexes while loading large amounts of data—provided the indexes are not needed by any other SQL statements in the meantime. This can unleash a dramatic speed-up which is visible in the chart and is, in fact, a common practice in data warehouses.

> **THINK ABOUT IT**
> How would Figure 8.1 change when using an index organized table or clustered index?
>
> Is there any indirect way an `insert` statement could possibly benefit from indexing? That is, could an additional index make an `insert` statement faster?

161

DELETE

Unlike the **insert** statement, the **delete** statement has a **where** clause that can use all the methods described in Chapter 2, *"The Where Clause"*, to benefit directly from indexes. In fact, the **delete** statement works like a **select** that is followed by an extra step to delete the identified rows.

The actual deletion of a row is a similar process to inserting a new one—especially the removal of the references from the indexes and the activities to keep the index trees in balance. The performance chart shown in Figure 8.2 is therefore very similar to the one shown for **insert**.

Figure 8.2. Delete Performance by Number of Indexes

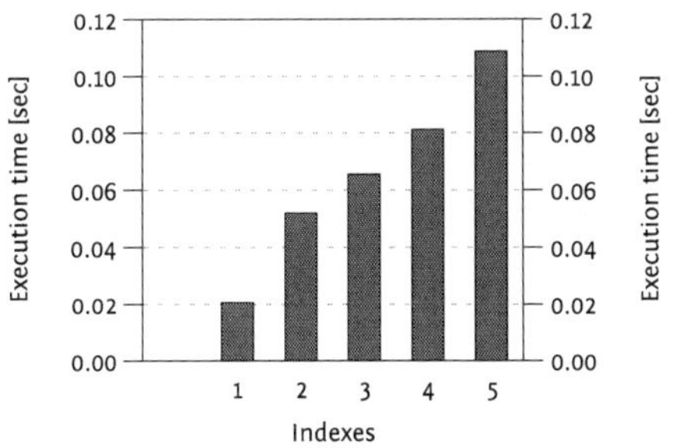

In theory, we would expect the best **delete** performance for a table without any indexes—as it is for **insert**. If there is no index, however, the database must read the full table to find the rows to be deleted. That means deleting the row would be fast but finding would be very slow. This case is therefore not shown in Figure 8.2.

Nevertheless it can make sense to execute a **delete** statement without an index just as it can make sense to execute a **select** statement without an index if it returns a large part of the table.

> **TIP**
>
> Even **delete** and **update** statements have an execution plan.

A `delete` statement without `where` clause is an obvious example in which the database cannot use an index, although this is a special case that has its own SQL command: `truncate table`. This command has the same effect as `delete` without `where` except that it deletes all rows in one shot. It is very fast but has two important side effects: (1) it does an implicit `commit` (exceptions: PostgreSQL and SQL Server); (2) it does not execute any triggers.

SIDE EFFECTS OF MVCC

Multiversion concurrency control (MVCC) is a database mechanism that enables non-blocking concurrent data access and a consistent transaction view. The implementations, however, differ from database to database and might even have considerable effects on performance.

The PostgreSQL database, for example, only keeps the version information (=visibility information) on the table level: deleting a row just sets the "deleted" flag in the table block. PostgreSQL's delete performance therefore *does not* depend on the number of indexes on the table. The physical deletion of the table row and the related index maintenance is carried out only during the VACUUM process.

UPDATE

An **update** statement must relocate the changed index entries to maintain the index order. For that, the database must remove the old entry and add the new one at the new location. The response time is basically the same as for the respective **delete** and **insert** statements together.

The **update** performance, just like **insert** and **delete**, also depends on the number of indexes on the table. The only difference is that **update** statements do not necessarily affect all columns because they often modify only a few selected columns. Consequently, an **update** statement does not necessarily affect all indexes on the table but only those that contain updated columns.

Figure 8.3 shows the response time for two **update** statements: one that sets all columns and affects all indexes and then a second one that updates a single column so it affects only one index.

Figure 8.3. Update Performance by Indexes and Column Count

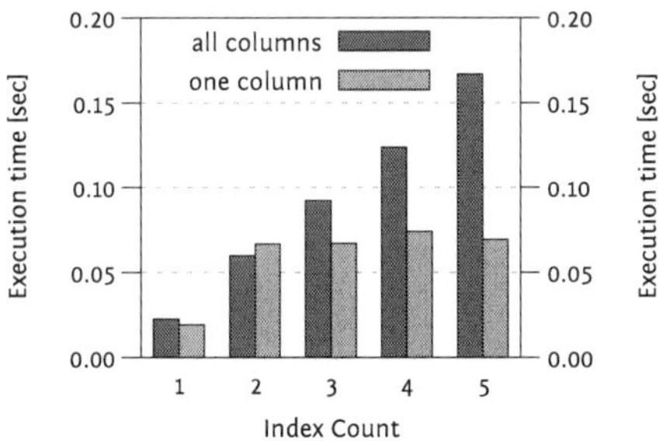

The **update** on all columns shows the same pattern we have already observed in the previous sections: the response time grows with each additional index. The response time of the **update** statement that affects only one index does not increase so much because it leaves most indexes unchanged.

To optimize **update** performance, you must take care to only update those columns that were changed. This is obvious if you write the **update** statement manually. ORM tools, however, might generate **update** statements that set all columns every time. Hibernate, for example, does this when disabling the *dynamic-update mode*. Since version 4.0, this mode is enabled by default.

When using ORM tools, it is a good practice to occasionally enable query logging in a development environment to verify the generated SQL statements. The tip entitled "Enabling SQL Logging" on page 95 has a short overview of how to enable SQL logging in some widely used ORM tools.

> **THINK ABOUT IT**
> Can you think of a case where **insert** or **delete** statements do not affect all indexes of a table?

Appendix A

Execution Plans

Before the database can execute an SQL statement, the optimizer has to create an execution plan for it. The database then executes this plan in a step-by-step manner. In this respect, the optimizer is very similar to a compiler because it translates the source code (SQL statement) into an executable program (execution plan).

The execution plan is the first place to look when searching for the cause of slow statements. The following sections explain how to retrieve and read an execution plan to optimize performance in various databases.

Contents

Oracle Database 166
    Getting an Execution Plan 166
    Operations 167
    Distinguishing Access and Filter-Predicates 170
PostgreSQL 172
    Getting an Execution Plan 172
    Operations 174
    Distinguishing Access and Filter-Predicates 177
SQL Server 180
    Getting an Execution Plan 180
    Operations 182
    Distinguishing Access and Filter-Predicates 185
MySQL 188
    Getting an Execution Plan 188
    Operations 188
    Distinguishing Access and Filter-Predicates 190

APPENDIX A: EXECUTION PLANS

ORACLE DATABASE

Most development environments (IDEs) can very easily show an execution plan but use very different ways to format them on the screen. The method described in this section delivers the execution plan as shown throughout the book and only requires the Oracle database in release 9*i*R2 or newer.

GETTING AN EXECUTION PLAN

Viewing an execution plan in the Oracle database involves two steps:

1. **explain plan for** — saves the execution plan in the PLAN_TABLE.

2. Format and display the execution plan.

CREATING AND SAVING AN EXECUTION PLAN

To create an execution plan, you just have to prefix the respective SQL statement with **explain plan for**:

EXPLAIN PLAN FOR select * from dual;

You can execute the **explain plan for** command in any development environment or SQL*Plus. It will, however, not show the plan but save it into a table named PLAN_TABLE. Starting with release 10*g*, this table is automatically available as a global temporary table. With previous releases, you have to create it in each schema as needed. Ask your database administrator to create it for you or to provide the **create table** statement from the Oracle database installation:

$ORACLE_HOME/rdbms/admin/utlxplan.sql

You can execute this statement in any schema you like to create the PLAN_TABLE in this schema.

> **WARNING**
>
> The **explain plan for** command does not necessarily create the same execution plan as though it would when executing the statement.

166

ORACLE OPERATIONS

SHOWING EXECUTION PLANS

The package DBMS_XPLAN was introduced with release 9*i*R2 and can format and display execution plans from the PLAN_TABLE. The following example shows how to display the last execution plan that was explained in the current database session:

```
select * from table(dbms_xplan.display);
```

Once again, if that statement doesn't work out of the box, you should ask your DBA for assistance.

The query will display the execution plan as shown in the book:

```
----------------------------------------------------------------
| Id | Operation          | Name | Rows | Bytes | Cost (%CPU)|.
----------------------------------------------------------------
|  0 | SELECT STATEMENT   |      |   1  |   2   |   2    (0)|.
|  1 |  TABLE ACCESS FULL | DUAL |   1  |   2   |   2    (0)|.
----------------------------------------------------------------
```

Some of the columns shown in this execution plan were removed in the book for a better fit on the page.

OPERATIONS

INDEX AND TABLE ACCESS

INDEX UNIQUE SCAN
> The INDEX UNIQUE SCAN performs the B-tree traversal only. The database uses this operation if a unique constraint ensures that the search criteria will match no more than one entry. See also Chapter 1, *"Anatomy of an Index"*.

INDEX RANGE SCAN
> The INDEX RANGE SCAN performs the B-tree traversal *and* follows the leaf node chain to find all matching entries. See also Chapter 1, *"Anatomy of an Index"*.

> The so-called index filter predicates often cause performance problems for an INDEX RANGE SCAN. The next section explains how to identify them.

167

APPENDIX A: EXECUTION PLANS

INDEX FULL SCAN

Reads the entire index—all rows—in index order. Depending on various system statistics, the database might perform this operation if it needs all rows in index order—e.g., because of a corresponding **order by** clause. Instead, the optimizer might also use an INDEX FAST FULL SCAN and perform an additional sort operation. See Chapter 6, *"Sorting and Grouping"*.

INDEX FAST FULL SCAN

Reads the entire index—all rows—as stored on the disk. This operation is typically performed instead of a full table scan if all required columns are available in the index. Similar to TABLE ACCESS FULL, the INDEX FAST FULL SCAN can benefit from multi-block read operations. See Chapter 5, *"Clustering Data"*.

TABLE ACCESS BY INDEX ROWID

Retrieves a row from the table using the ROWID retrieved from the preceding index lookup. See also Chapter 1, *"Anatomy of an Index"*.

TABLE ACCESS FULL

This is also known as full table scan. Reads the entire table—all rows and columns—as stored on the disk. Although multi-block read operations improve the speed of a full table scan considerably, it is still one of the most expensive operations. Besides high IO rates, a full table scan must inspect all table rows so it can also consume a considerable amount of CPU time. See also "Full Table Scan" on page 13.

JOINS

Generally join operations process only two tables at a time. In case a query has more joins, they are executed sequentially: first two tables, then the intermediate result with the next table. In the context of joins, the term "table" could therefore also mean "intermediate result".

NESTED LOOPS JOIN

Joins two tables by fetching the result from one table and querying the other table for each row from the first. See also "Nested Loops" on page 92.

HASH JOIN
The hash join loads the candidate records from one side of the join into a hash table that is then probed for each row from the other side of the join. See also "Hash Join" on page 101.

MERGE JOIN
The merge join combines two sorted lists like a zipper. Both sides of the join must be presorted. See also "Sort Merge" on page 109.

Sorting and Grouping

SORT ORDER BY
Sorts the result according to the **order by** clause. This operation needs large amounts of memory to materialize the intermediate result (not pipelined). See also "Indexing Order By" on page 130.

SORT ORDER BY STOPKEY
Sorts a subset of the result according to the **order by** clause. Used for top-N queries if pipelined execution is not possible. See also "Querying Top-N Rows" on page 143.

SORT GROUP BY
Sorts the result set on the **group by** columns and aggregates the sorted result in a second step. This operation needs large amounts of memory to materialize the intermediate result set (not pipelined). See also "Indexing Group By" on page 139.

SORT GROUP BY NOSORT
Aggregates a presorted set according the **group by** clause. This operation does not buffer the intermediate result: it is executed in a pipelined manner. See also "Indexing Group By" on page 139.

HASH GROUP BY
Groups the result using a hash table. This operation needs large amounts of memory to materialize the intermediate result set (not pipelined). The output is not ordered in any meaningful way. See also "Indexing Group By" on page 139.

TOP-N QUERIES

The efficiency of top-N queries depends on the execution mode of the underlying operations. They are very inefficient when aborting non-pipelined operations such as SORT ORDER BY.

COUNT STOPKEY
Aborts the underlying operations when the desired number of rows was fetched. See also the section called "Querying Top-N Rows".

WINDOW NOSORT STOPKEY
Uses a window function (**over** clause) to abort the execution when the desired number of rows was fetched. See also "Using Window Functions for Pagination" on page 156.

DISTINGUISHING ACCESS AND FILTER-PREDICATES

The Oracle database uses three different methods to apply **where** clauses (predicates):

ACCESS PREDICATE ("ACCESS")
The access predicates express the start and stop conditions of the leaf node traversal.

INDEX FILTER PREDICATE ("FILTER" FOR INDEX OPERATIONS)
Index filter predicates are applied during the leaf node traversal only. They do not contribute to the start and stop conditions and do not narrow the scanned range.

TABLE LEVEL FILTER PREDICATE ("FILTER" FOR TABLE OPERATIONS)
Predicates on columns that are not part of the index are evaluated on table level. For that to happen, the database must load the row from the table first.

ORACLE DISTINGUISHING ACCESS AND FILTER-PREDICATES

Execution plans that were created using the DBMS_XPLAN utility (see "Getting an Execution Plan" on page 166), show the index usage in the "Predicate Information" section below the tabular execution plan:

```
--------------------------------------------------------
| Id | Operation          | Name       | Rows  | Cost |
--------------------------------------------------------
|  0 | SELECT STATEMENT   |            |     1 | 1445 |
|  1 |  SORT AGGREGATE    |            |     1 |      |
|* 2 |   INDEX RANGE SCAN | SCALE_SLOW |  4485 | 1445 |
--------------------------------------------------------

Predicate Information (identified by operation id):
   2 - access("SECTION"=:A AND "ID2"=:B)
       filter("ID2"=:B)
```

The numbering of the predicate information refers to the "Id" column of the execution plan. There, the database also shows an asterisk to mark operations that have predicate information.

This example, taken from the chapter "Performance and Scalability", shows an INDEX RANGE SCAN that has access and filter predicates. The Oracle database has the peculiarity of also showing some filter predicate as access predicates—e.g., ID2=:B in the execution plan above.

> **IMPORTANT**
>
> If a condition shows up as filter predicate, it is a filter predicate—it does not matter if it is also shown as access predicate.

This means that the INDEX RANGE SCAN scans the entire range for the condition "SECTION"=:A and applies the filter "ID2"=:B on each row.

Filter predicates on table level are shown for the respective table access such as TABLE ACCESS BY INDEX ROWID or TABLE ACCESS FULL.

171

APPENDIX A: EXECUTION PLANS

PostgreSQL

The methods described in this section apply to PostgreSQL 8.0 and later.

Getting an Execution Plan

A PostgreSQL execution plan is fetched by putting the **explain** command in front of an SQL statement. There is, however, one important limitation: SQL statements with bind parameters (e.g., $1, $2, etc.) cannot be explained this way—they need to be prepared first:

```
PREPARE stmt(int) AS SELECT $1;
```

Note that PostgreSQL uses "$n" for bind parameters. Your database abstraction layer might hide this so you can use question marks as defined by the SQL standard.

The execution of the prepared statement can be explained:

```
EXPLAIN EXECUTE stmt(1);
```

Up till PostgreSQL 9.1, the execution plan was already created with the **prepare** call and could therefore not consider the actual values provided with **execute**. Since PostgreSQL 9.2 the creation of the execution plan is postponed until execution and thus can consider the actual values for the bind parameters.

> **Note**
>
> Statements without bind parameters can be explained directly:
>
> ```
> EXPLAIN SELECT 1;
> ```
>
> In this case, the optimizer has always considered the actual values during query planning. If you use PostgreSQL 9.1 or earlier and bind parameters in your program, you should also use **explain** with bind parameters to retrieve the same execution plan.

172

POSTGRESQL GETTING AN EXECUTION PLAN

The explain plan output is as follows:

```
                  QUERY PLAN
-------------------------------------------
 Result  (cost=0.00..0.01 rows=1 width=0)
```

The output has similar information as the Oracle execution plans shown throughout the book: the operation name ("Result"), the related cost, the row count estimate, and the expected row width.

Note that PostgreSQL shows two cost values. The first is the cost for the startup, the second is the total cost for the execution if all rows are retrieved. The Oracle database's execution plan only shows the second value.

The PostgreSQL **explain** command has two options. The VERBOSE option provides additional information like fully qualified table names — VERBOSE is usually not very valuable.

The second explain option is ANALYZE. Although it is widely used, I recommend not getting into the habit of using it automatically because it actually executes the statement. That is mostly harmless for **select** statements but it modifies your data when using it for **insert**, **update** or **delete**. To avoid the risk of accidentally modifying your data, you can enclose it in a transaction and perform a rollback afterwards.

The ANALYZE option executes the statement and records actual timing and row counts. That is valuable in finding the cause of incorrect cardinality estimates (row count estimates):

```
BEGIN;
EXPLAIN ANALYZE EXECUTE stmt(1);

                  QUERY PLAN
-------------------------------------------
 Result  (cost=0.00..0.01 rows=1 width=0)
         (actual time=0.002..0.002 rows=1 loops=1)
 Total runtime: 0.020 ms

ROLLBACK;
```

Note that the plan is formatted for a better fit on the page. PostgreSQL prints the "actual" values on the same line as the estimated values.

APPENDIX A: EXECUTION PLANS

> **WARNING**
>
> **explain analyze** executes the explained statement, even if the statement is an **insert, update** or **delete**.

The row count is the only value that is shown in both parts—in the estimated and in the actual figures. That allows you to quickly find erroneous cardinality estimates.

Last but not least, prepared statements must be closed again:

```
DEALLOCATE stmt;
```

OPERATIONS

INDEX AND TABLE ACCESS

SEQ SCAN
> The Seq Scan operation scans the entire relation (table) as stored on disk (like TABLE ACCESS FULL).

INDEX SCAN
> The Index Scan performs a B-tree traversal, walks through the leaf nodes to find all matching entries, and fetches the corresponding table data. It is like an INDEX RANGE SCAN followed by a TABLE ACCESS BY INDEX ROWID operation. See also Chapter 1, *"Anatomy of an Index"*.
>
> The so-called index filter predicates often cause performance problems for an Index Scan. The next section explains how to identify them.

INDEX ONLY SCAN (SINCE POSTGRESQL 9.2)
> The Index Only Scan performs a B-tree traversal and walks through the leaf nodes to find all matching entries. There is no table access needed because the index has all columns to satisfy the query (exception: MVCC visibility information). See also "Index-Only Scan" on page 116.

174

POSTGRESQL OPERATIONS

BITMAP INDEX SCAN / BITMAP HEAP SCAN / RECHECK COND
Tom Lane's post to the PostgreSQL performance mailing list is very clear and concise.

> A plain Index Scan fetches one tuple-pointer at a time from the index, and immediately visits that tuple in the table. A bitmap scan fetches all the tuple-pointers from the index in one go, sorts them using an in-memory "bitmap" data structure, and then visits the table tuples in physical tuple-location order.
>
> —Tom Lane[1]

JOIN OPERATIONS

Generally join operations process only two tables at a time. In case a query has more joins, they are executed sequentially: first two tables, then the intermediate result with the next table. In the context of joins, the term "table" could therefore also mean "intermediate result".

NESTED LOOPS
Joins two tables by fetching the result from one table and querying the other table for each row from the first. See also "Nested Loops" on page 92.

HASH JOIN / HASH
The hash join loads the candidate records from one side of the join into a hash table (marked with Hash in the plan) which is then probed for each record from the other side of the join. See also "Hash Join" on page 101.

MERGE JOIN
The (sort) merge join combines two sorted lists like a zipper. Both sides of the join must be presorted. See also "Sort Merge" on page 109.

---

[1] http://archives.postgresql.org/pgsql-performance/2005-12/msg00623.php

APPENDIX A: EXECUTION PLANS

SORTING AND GROUPING

SORT / SORT KEY

Sorts the set on the columns mentioned in Sort Key. The Sort operation needs large amounts of memory to materialize the intermediate result (not pipelined). See also "Indexing Order By" on page 130.

GROUPAGGREGATE

Aggregates a presorted set according to the **group by** clause. This operation does not buffer large amounts of data (pipelined). See also "Indexing Group By" on page 139.

HASHAGGREGATE

Uses a temporary hash table to group records. The HashAggregate operation does not require a presorted data set, instead it uses large amounts of memory to materialize the intermediate result (not pipelined). The output is not ordered in any meaningful way. See also "Indexing Group By" on page 139.

TOP-N QUERIES

LIMIT

Aborts the underlying operations when the desired number of rows has been fetched. See also "Querying Top-N Rows" on page 143.

The efficiency of the top-N query depends on the execution mode of the underlying operations. It is very inefficient when aborting non-pipelined operations such as Sort.

WINDOWAGG

Indicates the use of window functions. See also "Using Window Functions for Pagination" on page 156.

CAUTION

PostgreSQL cannot execute pipelined top-N queries when using window functions.

176

DISTINGUISHING ACCESS AND FILTER-PREDICATES

The PostgreSQL database uses three different methods to apply where clauses (predicates):

ACCESS PREDICATE ("INDEX COND")
The access predicates express the start and stop conditions of the leaf node traversal.

INDEX FILTER PREDICATE ("INDEX COND")
Index filter predicates are applied during the leaf node traversal only. They do not contribute to the start and stop conditions and do not narrow the scanned range.

TABLE LEVEL FILTER PREDICATE ("FILTER")
Predicates on columns that are not part of the index are evaluated on the table level. For that to happen, the database must load the row from the heap table first.

PostgreSQL execution plans do not show index access and filter predicates separately—both show up as "Index Cond". That means the execution plan must be compared to the index definition to differentiate access predicates from index filter predicates.

> **NOTE**
>
> The PostgreSQL explain plan does not provide enough information for finding index filter predicates.

The predicates shown as "Filter" are always table level filter predicates—even when shown for an Index Scan operation.

Consider the following example, which originally appeared in the "Performance and Scalability" chapter:

```
CREATE TABLE scale_data (
    section NUMERIC NOT NULL,
    id1     NUMERIC NOT NULL,
    id2     NUMERIC NOT NULL
);
CREATE INDEX scale_data_key ON scale_data(section, id1);
```

APPENDIX A: EXECUTION PLANS

The following **select** filters on the ID2 column, which is not included in the index:

```
PREPARE stmt(int) AS SELECT count(*)
                          FROM scale_data
                         WHERE section = 1
                           AND id2 = $1;
EXPLAIN EXECUTE stmt(1);

                          QUERY PLAN
-------------------------------------------------------
Aggregate  (cost=529346.31..529346.32 rows=1 width=0)
  Output: count(*)
  -> Index Scan using scale_data_key on scale_data
     (cost=0.00..529338.83 rows=2989 width=0)
     Index Cond: (scale_data.section = 1::numeric)
     Filter: (scale_data.id2 = ($1)::numeric)
```

The ID2 predicate shows up as "Filter" below the Index Scan operation. This is because PostgreSQL performs the table access as part of the Index Scan operation. In other words, the TABLE ACCESS BY INDEX ROWID operation of the Oracle database is hidden within PostgreSQL's Index Scan operation. It is therefore possible that a Index Scan filters on columns that are not included in the index.

IMPORTANT

The PostgreSQL Filter predicates are table level filter predicates — even when shown for an Index Scan.

When we add the index from the "Performance and Scalability" chapter, we can see that all columns show up as "Index Cond" — regardless of whether they are access or filter predicates.

```
CREATE INDEX scale_slow
        ON scale_data (section, id1, id2);
```

The execution plan with the new index does not show any filter conditions:

```
                          QUERY PLAN
-------------------------------------------------------
Aggregate  (cost=14215.98..14215.99 rows=1 width=0)
  Output: count(*)
  -> Index Scan using scale_slow on scale_data
     (cost=0.00..14208.51 rows=2989 width=0)
     Index Cond: (section = 1::numeric AND id2 = ($1)::numeric)
```

178

PostgreSQL Distinguishing Access and Filter-Predicates

Please note that the condition on ID2 cannot narrow the leaf node traversal because the index has the ID1 column before ID2. That means, the Index Scan will scan the entire range for the condition SECTION=1::numeric and apply the filter ID2=($1)::numeric on each row that fulfills the clause on SECTION.

SQL SERVER

The method described in this section applies to SQL Server Management Studio 2005 and later.

GETTING AN EXECUTION PLAN

With SQL Server, there are several ways to fetch an execution plan. The two most important methods are:

GRAPHICALLY
> The graphical representation of SQL Server execution plans is easily accessible in the Management Studio but is hard to share because the predicate information is only visible when the mouse is moved over the particular operation ("hover").

TABULAR
> The tabular execution plan is hard to read but easy to copy because it shows all relevant information at once.

GRAPHICALLY

The graphical explain plan is generated with one of the two buttons highlighted below.

The left button explains the highlighted statement directly. The right will capture the plan the next time a SQL statement is executed.

In both cases, the graphical representation of the execution plan appears in the "Execution plan" tab of the "Results" pane.

180

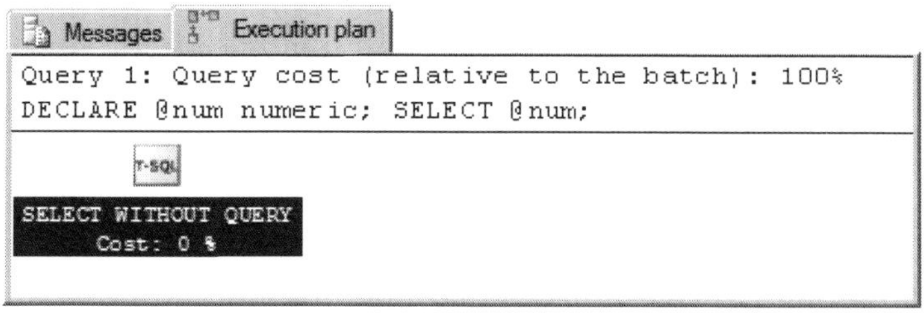

SQL SERVER GETTING AN EXECUTION PLAN

```
┌─────────────┬──────────────────┐
│ 🗐 Messages │ ⁸⁺ᵈ Execution plan │
├─────────────┴──────────────────┴────────────────────────┐
│ Query 1: Query cost (relative to the batch): 100%        │
│ DECLARE @num numeric; SELECT @num;                       │
│                                                           │
│            ┌──────┐                                       │
│            │T-SQL │                                       │
│            └──────┘                                       │
│      ┌────────────────────────┐                           │
│      │ SELECT WITHOUT QUERY    │                          │
│      │      Cost: 0 %          │                          │
│      └────────────────────────┘                           │
└───────────────────────────────────────────────────────────┘
```

The graphical representation is easy to read with a little bit of practice. Nonetheless, it only shows the most fundamental information: the operations and the table or index they act upon.

The Management Studio shows more information when moving the mouse over an operation (mouseover/hover). This makes it hard to share an execution plan with all its details.

TABULAR

The tabular representation of an SQL Server execution plan is fetched by profiling the execution of a statement. The following command enables it:

SET STATISTICS PROFILE ON

Once enabled, each executed statement produces an extra result set. select statements, for example, produce two result sets — the result of the statement first then the execution plan.

The tabular execution plan is hardly usable in SQL Server Management Studio because the StmtText is just too wide to fit on a screen.

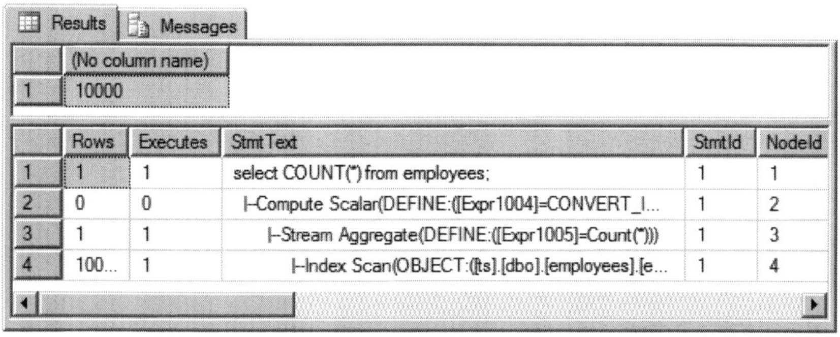

⊞ Results	🗐 Messages				
	(No column name)				
1	10000				

	Rows	Executes	StmtText	StmtId	NodeId
1	1	1	select COUNT(*) from employees;	1	1
2	0	0	|–Compute Scalar(DEFINE:([Expr1004]=CONVERT_I...	1	2
3	1	1	|–Stream Aggregate(DEFINE:([Expr1005]=Count(*)))	1	3
4	100...	1	|–Index Scan(OBJECT:([ts].[dbo].[employees].[e...	1	4

181

APPENDIX A: EXECUTION PLANS

The advantage of this representation is that it can be copied without loosing relevant information. This is very handy if you want to post an SQL Server execution plan on a forum or similar platform. In this case, it is often enough to copy the StmtText column and reformat it a little bit:

```
select COUNT(*) from employees;
  |--Compute Scalar(DEFINE:([Expr1004]=CONVERT_IMPLICIT(...))
      |--Stream Aggregate(DEFINE:([Expr1005]=Count(*)))
          |--Index Scan(OBJECT:([employees].[employees_pk]))
```

Finally, you can disable the profiling again:

```
SET STATISTICS PROFILE OFF
```

OPERATIONS

INDEX AND TABLE ACCESS

SQL Server has a simple terminology: "Scan" operations read the entire index or table while "Seek" operations use the B-tree or a physical address (RID, like Oracle ROWID) to access a specific part of the index or table.

INDEX SEEK, CLUSTERED INDEX SEEK
> The Index Seek performs a B-tree traversal *and* walks through the leaf nodes to find all matching entries. See also *"Anatomy of an Index"* on page 1.

INDEX SCAN, CLUSTERED INDEX SCAN
> Reads the entire index—all the rows—in the index order. Depending on various system statistics, the database might perform this operation if it needs all rows in index order—e.g., because of a corresponding **order by** clause.

KEY LOOKUP (CLUSTERED)
> Retrieves a single row from a clustered index. This is similar to Oracle INDEX UNIQUE SCAN for an Index-Organized-Table (IOT). See also *"Clustering Data"* on page 111.

SQL Server Operations

RID Lookup (Heap)

Retrieves a single row from a table—like Oracle TABLE ACCESS BY INDEX ROWID. See also *"Anatomy of an Index"* on page 1.

Table Scan

This is also known as full table scan. Reads the entire table—all rows and columns—as stored on the disk. Although multi-block read operations can improve the speed of a Table Scan considerably, it is still one of the most expensive operations. Besides high IO rates, a Table Scan must also inspect all table rows so it can also consume a considerable amount of CPU time. See also "Full Table Scan" on page 13.

Join Operations

Generally join operations process only two tables at a time. In case a query has more joins, they are executed sequentially: first two tables, then the intermediate result with the next table. In the context of joins, the term "table" could therefore also mean "intermediate result".

Nested Loops

Joins two tables by fetching the result from one table and querying the other table for each row from the first. SQL Server also uses the nested loops operation to retrieve table data after an index access. See also "Nested Loops" on page 92.

Hash Match

The hash match join loads the candidate records from one side of the join into a hash table which is then probed for each row from the other side of the join. See also "Hash Join" on page 101.

Merge Join

The merge join combines two sorted lists like a zipper. Both sides of the join must be presorted. See also "Sort Merge" on page 109.

Sorting and Grouping

Sort

> Sorts the result according to the **order by** clause. This operation needs large amounts of memory to materialize the intermediate result (not pipelined). See also "Indexing Order By" on page 130.

Sort (Top N Sort)

> Sorts a subset of the result according to the **order by** clause. Used for top-N queries if pipelined execution is not possible. See also "Querying Top-N Rows" on page 143.

Stream Aggregate

> Aggregates a presorted set according the **group by** clause. This operation does not buffer the intermediate result—it is executed in a pipelined manner. See also "Indexing Group By" on page 139.

Hash Match (Aggregate)

> Groups the result using a hash table. This operation needs large amounts of memory to materialize the intermediate result (not pipelined). The output is not ordered in any meaningful way. See also "Indexing Group By" on page 139.

Top-N Queries

Top

> Aborts the underlying operations when the desired number of rows has been fetched. See also "Querying Top-N Rows" on page 143.

> The efficiency of the top-N query depends on the execution mode of the underlying operations. It is very inefficient when aborting non-pipelined operations such as Sort.

Distinguishing Access and Filter-Predicates

The SQL Server database uses three different methods for applying **where** clauses (predicates):

ACCESS PREDICATE ("SEEK PREDICATES")
 The access predicates express the start and stop conditions of the leaf node traversal.

INDEX FILTER PREDICATE ("PREDICATES" OR "WHERE" FOR INDEX OPERATIONS)
 Index filter predicates are applied during the leaf node traversal only. They do not contribute to the start and stop conditions and do not narrow the scanned range.

TABLE LEVEL FILTER PREDICATE ("WHERE" FOR TABLE OPERATIONS)
 Predicates on columns which are not part of the index are evaluated on the table level. For that to happen, the database must load the row from the heap table first.

The following section explains how to identify filter predicates in SQL Server execution plans. It is based on the sample used to demonstrate the impact of index filter predicates in Chapter 3.

```
CREATE TABLE scale_data (
    section NUMERIC NOT NULL,
    id1     NUMERIC NOT NULL,
    id2     NUMERIC NOT NULL
);

CREATE INDEX scale_slow ON scale_data(section, id1, id2);
```

The sample statement selects by SECTION and ID2:

```
SELECT count(*)
  FROM scale_data
 WHERE section = @sec
   AND id2 = @id2
```

APPENDIX A: EXECUTION PLANS

IN GRAPHICAL EXECUTION PLANS

The graphical execution plan hides the predicate information in a tooltip that is only shown when moving the mouse over the Index Seek operation.

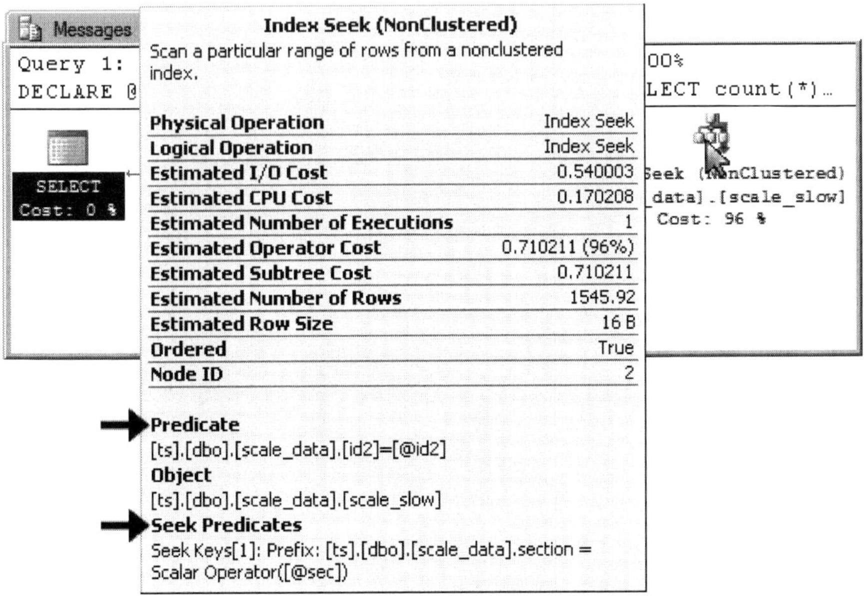

Index Seek (NonClustered)

Scan a particular range of rows from a nonclustered index.

Physical Operation	Index Seek
Logical Operation	Index Seek
Estimated I/O Cost	0.540003
Estimated CPU Cost	0.170208
Estimated Number of Executions	1
Estimated Operator Cost	0.710211 (96%)
Estimated Subtree Cost	0.710211
Estimated Number of Rows	1545.92
Estimated Row Size	16 B
Ordered	True
Node ID	2

Predicate
[ts].[dbo].[scale_data].[id2]=[@id2]
Object
[ts].[dbo].[scale_data].[scale_slow]
Seek Predicates
Seek Keys[1]: Prefix: [ts].[dbo].[scale_data].section =
Scalar Operator([@sec])

The SQL Server's *Seek Predicates* correspond to Oracle's access predicates—they narrow the leaf node traversal. Filter predicates are just labeled *Predicates* in SQL Server's graphical execution plan.

186

In Tabular Execution Plans

Tabular execution plans have the predicate information in the same column in which the operations appear. It is therefore very easy to copy and past all the relevant information in one go.

```
DECLARE @sec numeric;
DECLARE @id2 numeric;

SET STATISTICS PROFILE ON

SELECT count(*)
  FROM scale_data
 WHERE section = @sec
   AND id2 = @id2

SET STATISTICS PROFILE OFF
```

The execution plan is shown as a second result set in the results pane. The following is the StmtText column—with a little reformatting for better reading:

```
|--Compute Scalar(DEFINE:([Expr1004]=CONVERT_IMPLICIT(...))
    |--Stream Aggregate(DEFINE:([Expr1008]=Count(*)))
        |--Index Seek(OBJECT:([scale_data].[scale_slow]),
           SEEK: ([scale_data].[section]=[@sec])
                 ORDERED FORWARD
           WHERE:([scale_data].[id2]=[@id2]))
```

The SEEK label introduces access predicates, the WHERE label marks filter predicates.

APPENDIX A: EXECUTION PLANS

MySQL

The method described in this section applies to all versions of MySQL.

Getting an Execution Plan

Put **explain** in front of an SQL statement to retrieve the execution plan.

EXPLAIN SELECT 1;

The plan is shown in tabular form (some less important columns removed):

```
~+-------+------+---------------+------+~+------+-----------~
~| table | type | possible_keys | key  |~| rows | Extra
~+-------+------+---------------+------+~+------+-----------~
~| NULL  | NULL | NULL          | NULL |~| NULL | No tables...
~+-------+------+---------------+------+~+------+-----------~
```

The most important information is in the TYPE column. Although the MySQL documentation refers to it as "join type", I prefer to describe it as "access type" because it actually specifies how the data is accessed. The meaning of the type value is described in the next section.

Operations

Index and Table Access

MySQL's explain plan tends to give a false sense of safety because it says so much about indexes being used. Although technically correct, it does not mean that it is using the index efficiently. The most important information is in the TYPE column of the MySQL's **explain** output—but even there, the keyword INDEX doesn't indicate proper indexing.

188

MySQL Operations

EQ_REF, CONST

Performs a B-tree traversal to find *one* row (like INDEX UNIQUE SCAN) and fetches additional columns from the table if needed (TABLE ACCESS BY INDEX ROWID). The database uses this operation if a primary key or unique constraint ensures that the search criteria will match no more than one entry. See "Using Index" to check whether the table access happens or not.

REF, RANGE

Performs a B-tree traversal, walks through the leaf nodes to find all matching index entries (similar to INDEX RANGE SCAN) and fetches additional columns from the primary table store if needed (TABLE ACCESS BY INDEX ROWID). See "Using Index" to check whether the table access happens or not.

INDEX

Reads the entire index—all rows—in the index order (similar to INDEX FULL SCAN).

ALL

Reads the entire table—all rows and columns—as stored on the disk. Besides high IO rates, a table scan must also inspect all rows from the table so that it can also put a considerable load on the CPU. See also "Full Table Scan" on page 13.

USING INDEX (IN THE "EXTRA" COLUMN)

When the "Extra" column shows "Using Index", it means that the table is not accessed because the index has all the required data. Think of "using index ONLY". However, if a clustered index is used (e.g., the PRIMARY index when using InnoDB) "Using Index" does not appear in the Extra column although it is technically an Index-Only Scan. See also "*Clustering Data*" on page 111.

PRIMARY (IN THE "KEY" OR "POSSIBLE_KEYS" COLUMN)

PRIMARY is the name of the automatically created index for the primary key.

APPENDIX A: EXECUTION PLANS

SORTING AND GROUPING

USING FILESORT (IN THE "EXTRA" COLUMN)
"using filesort" in the Extra column indicates an explicit sort operation—no matter where the sort takes place (main memory or on disk). "Using filesort" needs large amounts of memory to materialize the intermediate result (not pipelined). See also "Indexing Order By" on page 130.

TOP-N QUERIES

IMPLICIT: NO "USING FILESORT" IN THE "EXTRA" COLUMN
A MySQL execution plan does not show a top-N query explicitly. If you are using the limit syntax and don't see "using filesort" in the extra column, it is executed in a pipelined manner. See also "Querying Top-N Rows" on page 143.

DISTINGUISHING ACCESS AND FILTER-PREDICATES

The MySQL database uses three different ways to evaluate where clauses (predicates):

ACCESS PREDICATE (VIA THE "KEY_LEN" COLUMN)
The access predicates express the start and stop conditions of the leaf node traversal.

INDEX FILTER PREDICATE ("USING INDEX CONDITION", SINCE MYSQL 5.6)
Index filter predicates are applied during the leaf node traversal only. They do not contribute to the start and stop conditions and do not narrow the scanned range.

TABLE LEVEL FILTER PREDICATE ("USING WHERE" IN THE "EXTRA" COLUMN)
Predicates on columns which are not part of the index are evaluated on the table level. For that to happen, the database must load the row from the table first.

MySQL execution plans do not show which predicate types are used for each condition—they just list the predicate types in use.

190

MYSQL DISTINGUISHING ACCESS AND FILTER-PREDICATES

In the following example, the entire **where** clause is used as access predicate:

```
CREATE TABLE demo (
    id1 NUMERIC
  , id2 NUMERIC
  , id3 NUMERIC
  , val NUMERIC);

INSERT INTO demo VALUES (1,1,1,1);
INSERT INTO demo VALUES (2,2,2,2);

CREATE INDEX demo_idx
         ON demo
            (id1, id2, id3);

EXPLAIN
 SELECT *
   FROM demo
  WHERE id1=1
    AND id2=1;

+------+----------+---------+------+-------+
| type | key      | key_len | rows | Extra |
+------+----------+---------+------+-------+
| ref  | demo_idx | 12      |   1  |       |
+------+----------+---------+------+-------+
```

There is no "Using where" or "Using index condition" shown in the "Extra" column. The index is, however, used (type=ref, key=demo_idx) so you can assume that the entire **where** clause qualifies as access predicate.

You can use the key_len value to verify this. It shows that the query uses the first 12 bytes of the index definition. To map this to column names, you "just" need to know how much storage space each column needs (see "Data Type Storage Requirements" in the MySQL documentation). In absence of a NOT NULL constraint, MySQL needs an extra byte for each column. After all, each NUMERIC column needs 6 bytes in the example. Therefore, the key length of 12 confirms that the first two index columns are used as access predicates.

191

APPENDIX A: EXECUTION PLANS

When filtering with the ID3 column (instead of the ID2) MySQL 5.6 and later use an index filter predicate ("Using index condition"):

```
EXPLAIN
  SELECT *
    FROM demo
   WHERE id1=1
     AND id3=1;

+------+----------+---------+------+----------------------+
| type | key      | key_len | rows | Extra                |
+------+----------+---------+------+----------------------+
| ref  | demo_idx | 6       |    1 | Using index condition |
+------+----------+---------+------+----------------------+
```

In this case, the key length of six means only one column is used as access predicate.

Previous versions of MySQL used a table level filter predicate for this query—identified by "Using where" in the "Extra" column:

```
+------+----------+---------+------+-------------+
| type | key      | key_len | rows | Extra       |
+------+----------+---------+------+-------------+
| ref  | demo_idx | 6       |    1 | Using where |
+------+----------+---------+------+-------------+
```

192

Index

Symbols

2PC, *89*
?, :var, @var (see bind parameter)

A

Access Predicate, *44*
access predicates
    recognizing in execution plans
        Oracle, *170*
        PostgreSQL, *177*
        SQL Server, *185*
adaptive cursor sharing (Oracle), *75*
auto parameterization (SQL Server), *39*

B

B-tree (balanced search tree), *4*
between, *44*
bind parameter, *32*
    contraindications
        histograms, *34*
        LIKE filters, *47*
        partitions, *35*
    for execution plan caching, *32*
    type safety, *66*
bind peeking (Oracle), *75*
bitmap index, *50*
Bitmap Index Scan (PostgreSQL), *175*
Brewer's CAP theorem, *89*

C

CAP theorem, *89*
cardinality estimate, *27*
CBO (see optimizer, cost based)
clustered index, *122*
    transform to SQL Server heap table, *127*
clustering factor, *21*, *114*
    automatically optimized, *133*
clustering key, *123*
collation, *24*
commit
    deferrable constraints, *11*
    implicit for **truncate table**, *163*
    two phase, *89*
compiling, *18*
computed columns (SQL Server), *27*
constraint
    deferrable, *11*
    NOT NULL, *56*
cost value, *18*

count(*)
    often as index-only scan, *120*
    Oracle requires NOT NULL constraint, *57*
COUNT STOPKEY, *145*
cursor sharing (Oracle), *39*

D

data transport object (DTO), *105*
DATE
    efficiently working with, *62*
DBMS_XPLAN, *167*
DEALLOCATE, *174*
DEFERRABLE constraint, *11*
DETERMINISTIC (Oracle), *30*
distinct, *97*
distinct()
    in JPA and Hibernate, *97*
DML, *159*
doubly linked list, *2*
dynamic-update (Hibernate), *164*

E

eager fetching, *96*
eventual consistency, *89*
execution plan, *10*, *165*
    cache, *32*, *75*
    creating
        MySQL, *188*
        Oracle, *166*
        PostgreSQL, *172*
        SQL Server, *180*
    operations
        MySQL, *188*
        Oracle, *167*
        PostgreSQL, *174*
        SQL Server, *182*
explain
    MySQL, *188*
    Oracle, *166*
    PostgreSQL, *172*

F

FBI (see index, function-based)
FETCH ALL PROPERTIES (HQL), *105*
fetch first, *144*
filter predicates
    effects (chart), *81*
    recognizing in execution plans
        Oracle, *170*
        PostgreSQL, *177*
        SQL Server, *185*

193

full table scan, *13*
    All (MySQL), *189*
    Seq Scan (PostgreSQL), *174*
    TABLE ACCESS FULL (Oracle), *168*
    Table Scan (SQL Server), *183*
functions, *24*
    deterministic, *29*
        in partial indexes, *52*
    window, *156*

G

group by, *139*
    with PostrgesSQL and the Oracle
    database and an ASC/DESC index not
    pipelined, *140*

H

hash join, *101*
HASH GROUP BY, *169*
HASH JOIN (Oracle), *169*
HASH Join (PostgreSQL), *175*
Hash Match, *183*
Hash Match (Aggregate), *184*
heap table, *3*, *122*
    creating in SQL Server, *127*
Hibernate
    eager fetching, *96*
    ILIKE uses LOWER, *98*
    updates all columns, *164*
hint, *19*

I

IMMUTABLE (PostgreSQL), *30*
index
    covering, *117*
    fulltext, *48*
    function-based, *24*
        case insensitive, *24*
        to index mathematical
        calculations, *77*
    join, *50*
    limits
        MySQL, Oracle, PostgreSQL, *121*
        SQL Server, *122*
    merge, *49*
    multi-column, *12*
        wrong order (effects), *81*
    partial, *51*
    prefix (MySQL), *121*
    secondary, *123*
index in MySQL execution plans, *189*
index-only scan, *116*
index-organized table, *122*
    database support, *127*
Index Cond (PostgreSQL), *177*
INDEX FAST FULL SCAN, *168*

INDEX FULL SCAN, *168*
Index Only Scan (PostgreSQL), *174*
INDEX RANGE SCAN, *167*
Index Scan (PostgreSQL), *174*
Index Seek, *182*
INDEX UNIQUE SCAN, *167*
    when accessing an IOT, *124*
INTERNAL_FUNCTION, *67*
IOT (index-organized table), *122*

J

join, *91*
    full outer, *109*

K

Key Lookup (Clustered), *182*

L

lazy fetching
    for scalar attributes (columns), *104*
leaf node, *2*
    split, *160*
LIKE, *45*
    alternatives, *48*
    as index filter predicate, *112*
    on DATE column, *67*
    on DATE columns, *67*
limit (MySQL, PostgreSQL), *144*
logarithmic scalability, *7*
LOWER, *24*

M

Merge Join, *109*
    PostgreSQL, *175*
    SQL Server, *183*
MERGE JOIN (Oracle), *169*
multi-block read
    for a full table scan, *13*
    for a INDEX FAST FULL SCAN, *168*
MVCC, *163*
    affects PostgreSQL index-only scan, *174*
myths
    dynamic SQL is slow, *72*, *74*
    most selective column first
        disproof, *43*
        origin, *49*
    Oracle cannot index NULL, *56*

N

N+1 problem, *92*
Nested Loops, *92*
    PostgreSQL, *175*
    SQL Server, *183*
NESTED LOOPS (Oracle), *168*

NOSORT
    SORT GROUP BY, *140*
    WINDOW, *157*
NULL
    indexing in Oracle, *54*

O

offset (MySQL, PostgreSQL), *148*
optimizer, *18*
    cost based, *18*
    hint, *19*
    rule based, *18*
    statistics, *21*
OPTIMIZE FOR (SQL Server), *76*
OPTION (SQL Server), *76*
OR
    to disable filters, *72*
order by, *130*
    ASC, DESC, *134*
    NULLS FIRST/LAST, *137*
    support matrix, *138*
OVER(), *156*

P

paging, *147*
    offset method, *148*
    seek method, *149*
        approximated, *152*
parameter sniffing (SQL Server), *76*
parsing, *18*
partial index, *51*
partial objects (ORM), *104*
partitions and bind parameters, *35*
pipelining, *92*
PLAN_TABLE, *166*
predicate information, *20*
    access vs. filter predicates, *44*
    in execution plans
        MySQL, *190*
        Oracle, *170*
        SQL Server, *185*
prepare (PostgreSQL), *172*
primary key w/o unique index, *11*

Q

query planner (see optimizer)

R

RBO (see optimizer, rule based)
RECOMPILE (SQL Server hint), *76*
result set transformer, *98*
RID, *3*
RID Lookup (Heap), *183*
root node, *5*
    split, *160*

row sequencing, *113*
row values, *153*
ROWID, *3*
ROWNUM (Oracle pseudo column), *144*, *148*
ROW_NUMBER, *156*

S

scalability, *81*
    horizontal, *87*
    logarithmic, *7*
Scalability, *79*
Seek Predicates (SQL Server), *185*
select *, avoid to
    enable index-only scans, *120*
    improve hash join performance, *104*
Seq Scan, *174*
Sort (SQL Server), *184*
SORT GROUP BY, *169*
    NOSORT, *140*
SORT ORDER BY, *130*
    STOPKEY, *145*
SQL area, *75*
SQL injection, *32*
SSD (Solid State Disk), *90*
statistics, *21*
    for Oracle function-based indexes, *28*
STATISTICS PROFILE, *181*
STOPKEY
    COUNT, *145*
    SORT ORDER BY, *146*
    WINDOW, *157*
Stream Aggregate, *184*

T

top (SQL Server), *145*
Top-N Query, *143*
TO_CHAR(DATE), *66*
TRUNC(DATE), *62*
truncate table, *163*
    triggers not executed, *163*

U

UPPER, *24*

V

Vacuum (PostgreSQL), *163*
virtual columns for NOT NULL constraints
on FBI, *58*

W

where, *9*
    conditional, *72*
    in SQL Server execution plan, *187*
window functions, *156*

MORE FROM MARKUS WINAND

The only thing better than the book ...

    ... is my training. Whether an one-on-one online course or a group training presented on-site, it's sure to be an experience rich in beneficial and long-lasting effects.

                                        http://winand.at/training

Durable solutions ...

    ... are available for single queries or entire databases. My index design ensures performance for many years to come.

                                    http://winand.at/index-design

Modern SQL ...

    ... is my upcoming book. Because a lot has changed since SQL-92! You can check it out online now and subscribe the newsletter to get the new chapters too.

                                        http://modern-sql.com/

You'll find information on everything I offer on my website:

http://winand.at/